Integration of handicapped children in society

Integration of handicapped children in society

Edited by
James Loring and Graham Burn

London, Henley and Boston
Routledge & Kegan Paul
in association with
The Spastics Society

First published in 1975
by Routledge & Kegan Paul Ltd
39, Store Street
London WC1E 7DD.
Broadway House, Newtown Road,
Henley-on-Thames RG9 1EN.
9 Park Street,
Boston, Mass. 02108, USA
Set in IBM Century.
Printed in Great Britain by
Unwin Brothers Ltd
Reprinted 1976.

ISBN 0 7100 8269 X

Contents

Contributors   ix

Introduction   xiii

1   Social aspects of integration
Margaret R. Morgan   1

2   A research study on the integration of
physically handicapped children in ordinary
primary schools
Elizabeth Anderson   10

3   The future place of the handicapped in
society
Jack Tizard   22

4   An exercise in integration
Pauline Skelly   29

5   Designing for physically handicapped
children — are you on the right level,
Mr Architect?
Brian Goldsmith   36

Contents

6 The problem of the multiple-handicapped child
James Loring 49

7 Preparing handicapped children for life
Anita Loring 57

8 An individual programme for behaviour modification
Lillemor Jernqvist 72

9 Integration of the maladjusted
John Wilson 80

10 Emotional problems of the limb deficient child
Ian Fletcher 87

11 Physically handicapped children in an ordinary primary school — a new dimension
K.W. Foster 90

12 Visually handicapped children in the infant school
Heather Jones 102

13 The social and educational problems of the young spina bifida child
K.M. Laurence and E.R. Laurence 109

14 The teacher and the handicapped child
D.N. Thomas 134

15 The multi-handicapped child in a boarding school for cerebral palsy
R.A. Pedder 143

Contents

16 The special school as a normalising agency
    D. Braybrook   155

17 Integrating handicapped children into
    ordinary secondary schools
    C.L. Frost   163

18 Description of a current survey of disabled
    students at universities and polytechnics in
    Great Britain
    Alan Chamberlain   168

19 A philosophy for life for 16-25-year-old
    physically handicapped children
    Marc Gicquiaud   180

20 The young adult and his desire for
    integration
    E.E. Doherty   191

21 A consumer's viewpoint
    June Maelzer   201

22 To be in society or to be beside it
    Gun Andersson   209

Contributors

Margaret Morgan, MBE, MIPM
Head of Social Work and Employment Department, The
Spastics Society

Elizabeth Anderson, MA, BSc
Research Officer, Thomas Coram Research Unit in the
University of London Institute of Education

Jack Tizard, CBE, PhD
Research Professor of Child Development and Director of
Thomas Coram Research Unit in the University of London
Institute of Education

Pauline Skelly
Headmistress, Dovecot County Primary School, Liverpool

Brian Goldsmith, ARIBA, AIOB, MSIA
Senior Architect of Sir Hugh Wilson and Lewis Womersley,
London

James Loring
Director, The Spastics Society and Secretary General, The
International Cerebral Palsy Society

Contributors

Anita Loring
Secretary, The International Cerebral Palsy Society.
Formerly Research Associate, Farmington Trust Research
Unit, Oxford

Lillemor Jernqvist, BA Psych
Bräcke Östergård, Gothenburg, Sweden

John Wilson, MA
University of Oxford Department of Educational Studies

Ian Fletcher, MRCS, LRCP
Medical Officer, Department of Health and Social Security

Kenneth Foster, LCP, FRGS
Headmaster, Twydall County Primary School, Gillingham,
Kent

Heather Jones
Senior Education Adviser and Parent Counsellor, Royal
National Institute for the Blind, Lickey Grange School, Old
Birmingham Road, Bromsgrove, Worcs

K. Michael Laurence, MA, MB, CLB, FRC Path
Reader in Applied Genetics, Department of Child Health, The
Welsh National School of Medicine

Rose Laurence, BA
Department of Child Health, The Welsh National School of
Medicine

David N. Thomas, Certificate in Education of Handicapped
Children
Organising Tutor and Head of Department for Special
Education, City of Leicester College of Education

Robert Pedder, JP
Headmaster, The Wilfred Pickles School, Duddington, Lincs

David Braybrook, Teachers' Certificate, Oxford, Certificate
for Teachers of the Deaf, Manchester
Lecturer, Lady Spencer Churchill College of Education,
Oxford

C. Leslie Frost, LLB, ACP Diploma in Academic Studies
Assistant Education Officer (Special Education), City of
Sheffield

Alan Chamberlain, BA
Assistant Secretary, Council of Post Office Unions. Formerly
Research Officer, National Innovations Centre

Marc Gicquiaud, MD
Director, 'Les Templiers', Cornusse, France

Edward Doherty, MA, B Mus
Principal, Oakwood Further Education Centre, Kelvedon,
Essex

June Maelzer, BSc Psych
Warden, Wolsley Street Hostel, Birmingham

Gun Andersson
Special Education Counsellor, Malmö, Sweden

Introduction

Many handicapped children have been and are being educated in ordinary schools. How many more can ordinary schools, many of which are at the moment experiencing great difficulties of their own, absorb, and what changes in philosophy and physical facilities are necessary? Contributions in this book, which come from many countries, throw valuable light on these most intricate problems.

I express my gratitude to Graham Burn for his work on this book, and to my wife, Anita Loring, who directed the International Study Group which was made possible by the joint sponsorship of the International Cerebral Palsy Society and the Spastics Society.

James Loring

1
Social aspects of integration

Margaret R. Morgan

I have been given a delightfully general title for my paper, so
I plan to discuss a topic which interests me particularly and
which I hope will stimulate discussion, that of attitudes to
disability, the effects these attitudes have on handicapped
children and young people, and the ways in which these may
help or hinder social integration.

I plan to take a critical — sometimes self-critical — but, I
hope, positive line. However, I would like to make it clear
that my criticisms are not directed to any one profession or
group of people. Most apply to all of us, in whatever field
we work, and I think it behoves each of us to question ourselves and our own attitudes, both to the disabled as a group
and also to individual disabled people.

At the present time there seems to be a good deal of
specious, glib and often hypocritical talk about social
acceptance and integration of disabled people which is not
borne out in practice and which includes a superficial and
often false denial of the differences between those who are
demonstrably handicapped and most other people. People
talk in encouraging terms about everyone being handicapped
in one way or other, and speakers sometimes draw attention
to their own handicaps to prove the point. This may well be
true, as none of us meet up to the image of a Venus or an
Adonis, but it is not always relevant or helpful to over-
simplify the problems in this way. A more honest appraisal

1

Margaret R. Morgan

and recognition of the differences may lead to more genuine understanding and empathy. Disabled people, too, often make a plea to be accepted as though there were no impediments at all, and this can create practical difficulties and embarrassment that may inhibit people from offering necessary assistance and support. Perhaps it would be better to seek acceptance as they are in reality, which may be different, sometimes very different, from the average but, none the less, claiming the same basic rights as any other man or woman.

I have chosen to use the word 'disabled' rather than 'handicapped' up to now, because an impairment or disability is not necessarily, or always, handicapping. Whether a particular impairment constitutes a handicap to an individual child, adolescent or adult is the result of a complex of highly personal and environmental factors, and no clear-cut guide lines can be laid down. I hope in this short paper to look at how far education (in its broadest sense), personal and family relationships and general attitudes can combine to help or hinder a disabled person in achieving acceptance in the community (a phrase which I much prefer to 'integration').

1   Some disabled people make use of their handicap. Instead of playing it down or denying the reality of it, they acknowledge and even stress or exaggerate the handicap to obtain or maintain help, attention or affection. An extreme form of this way of coping with the disability is begging, which is displaying the handicap in a public and open way to arouse compassion, guilt or disgust and other strong and conflicting emotions, to motivate the viewer or passer-by to give money or services. Although overt begging is now only found in countries with very inadequate social services, there are many subtler forms of begging which are used in more sophisticated societies to produce the same results. Groups of kindly people trailing round schools and residential centres for disabled children and adults, viewing the work — and people — and seeing how their money is spent, and at the

2

same time being stimulated to give more; publicity highlight-
ing or exaggerating people's financial or social hardships: these
are really civilised forms of begging. All this may be very
necessary where fund-raising and public interest are concerned, but we must also accept that these activities probably
have a cumulative, as well as an individual, effect on the
attitudes of disabled children and adults, even though some
of it may be at a subconscious level.

I am not suggesting that there is necessarily anything
unethical in using the handicap, either in a positive way by
publicising every little achievement, or in a negative way by
drawing attention to the pathos and inadequacy of the
disabled person, to help improve conditions and services for
either an individual or group of people. We do need, however,
to acknowledge and recognise that in using people for
publicity or display in this way we are affecting their self-
image and their attitudes to their disabilities and we could
well be impeding their acceptance into the community.

We have to accept, too, that some parents, and probably
mothers, in particular, may prolong the dependence and
emphasise the disability of a handicapped child or adolescent
in order to meet their own need, either to go on mothering
or perhaps even to become a 'martyr to the cause'. Does this
ever happen to people other than parents who are looking
after handicapped children, I wonder?

2   I would now like to turn to the opposite extreme, that
of denial of disability or of its handicapping effects. As I
said earlier in this paper, there is a current tendency in some
circles to pretend — and I mean pretend — that there is no
difference between some obviously physically or intellectually impaired people and the able-bodied population at large.
This seems to be both dishonest and unhelpful and it must
cause a good deal of confusion to children and adolescents
who are fully aware of differences which other people do
not seem able to admit or recognise openly.

3

Even if the reality of the disability is acknowledged, we so often expect handicapped children and adolescents to pretend that it does not affect them and to exhibit a cheerful, accepting and grateful attitude at all times. In fact, we only allow disabled people (with any degree of real handicap) to become integrated on strictly regulated conditions, most of which involve a good deal of denial and conformation to quite rigid stereotypes. Here I would like to draw your attention to a quite significant published report on the attitude of nurses to their patients in a London hospital (Felicity Stockwell, *The Unpopular Patient*, Royal College of Nursing, 1973).

In this study, the nurses' attitudes to their patients were analysed and the patients that the nurses most and least enjoyed caring for were identified and their behaviour observed. I would like to quote from this report, as the findings seem relevant to this paper:

Patients the nurses enjoyed caring for:
Were able to communicate readily with the nurses.
Knew the nurses' names.
Were able to joke and laugh with the nurses.
Co-operated in being helped to get well and expressed determination to do so (p.46).

Patients the nurses least enjoyed caring for:
Grumbled and complained.
Communicated lack of enjoyment at being in hospital.
Implied that they were suffering more than was believed by the nurses.
Suffered from conditions the nurses felt could be better cared for in other wards or specialized hospitals (p.49).

The majority of nurses included among the reasons given for choosing the patient for whom they most enjoyed caring, some reference to the patients being fun, having

a good sense of humour, being easy to get on with and friendly.
Some individual preferences related to how well the nurses knew the patient.
Very few of the reasons given related to the nursing needs of the patients (p.49).
Frustration and impatience were expressed about patients who grumble, moan or demand attention, also irritation about patients considered to be wasting their time.
Psychiatric patients were overtly rejected or ridiculed (p.51).
Many of the interactions in the wards were conducted in a joking, teasing or bantering manner. There were a few patients and a few nurses who were particularly adept at initiating interactions of this sort, but other people would join in fairly readily (p.56).
Joking, teasing and bantering interchange was common in the three medical wards.
Jocular grumbling, which occurred most among ambulant patients, appeared to limit formal complaining.
Teasing and banter were used in different ways with popular and less popular patients (p.58).

It seems, therefore, that in order to gain the nurses' approval, and often their nursing care and attention, the patient had to enjoy being in hospital and to joke and make light of his illness. In fact, to ingratiate oneself with the nurses seems to have been the most obvious way of gaining popularity.

This seems a rather startling, though in many ways understandable, revelation of how nurses cope with their own stresses and strains and I think that there are some direct parallels with the ways in which all of us deal with our ambivalent attitudes towards disabled people. In order to be accepted and to be considered as socially integrated, disabled people, on the whole, have to pretend that their disability does not really affect them, they must joke and be cheerful

and, in the same way as patients in hospital, ingratiate themselves in order to get attention. If they do not behave in this
way, many able-bodied people find the reality and burden of
the handicap intolerable to bear. Another way of dealing
with the problem of personal relationships is to pretend that
disabled people are perpetual Peter Pans who never grow up
and this attitude, somehow, absolves one from attempting
to make any kind of adult relationship with a disabled person.

Our general attitudes to young people in their formative
years are, of course, crucial, but I wonder sometimes whether
what we see as good and acceptable attributes are necessarily
appropriate for adolescents who, as a normal and essential
part of their development, go through very difficult, aggressive, antisocial and anti-authority phases in their search for
their emerging adult personalities.

Last summer, I visited a special residential school for
their Speech Day and Annual Sports. The Chairman, in
making his address to the audience of parents, children and
other interested visitors, commented on what a happy school
it was, and how cheerful the children were all the time. This
school contained quite a large number of adolescent boys
and girls with very special problems and handicaps and it
seemed to me unnatural either to expect or want these young
people to be happy and smiling all the time. Clearly, one
wants a school to be a positive, relaxed and cheerful place,
but do we ever allow our teenagers to be depressed and
angry and miserable? Or is this too difficult to face, because
we can only cope with a handicapped person who is accepting,
grateful, childlike and happy?

3   I would now like to turn to the middle way, which I see
as a realistic coming to terms with the disability. I deliber-
ately use the phrase 'coming to terms with' rather than
'acceptance of' because I question whether anyone, parent
or disabled man or woman, ever really accepts the situation,
and if they did, I imagine that many would give up the

unequal struggle. But coming to terms with the reality of the disability and the limitations that it may impose is altogether different. It can imply a certain measure of 'using' the disability to obtain the help and support that is needed and also some 'denial' too, so that you are left with goals to strive for and perhaps to achieve, to prove other people wrong!

Here I would like to expand a little on the question of stereotypes and their effect on our attitudes towards the education and training of handicapped children and young people. We are very much influenced by what is generally expected of certain groups of people, and especially of groups of stigmatised and minority groups, like the disabled. For instance, we have a mental image of a blind person with a white, tapping stick and dark glasses, who has an additional hearing gift to compensate for his blindness, yet we know from what blind people tell us that they are as varied in their gifts, skills and problems as any other group of the population. A deaf person, too, evokes a picture of a somewhat comic and irritating man who is aggressive and difficult and who always feels that other people are talking about him. Retarded people are nearly always seen as smiling, cheerful, chubby mongols, whereas there are very many variations in people who have intellectual handicaps. Those who are epileptic are usually pictured as being heavy, dull, bad-tempered and unattractive people and this is certainly not true of the majority. Where there is a physical handicap, the image is conjured up of a pretty smiling little girl, passively sitting in a wheelchair or, alternatively, one of a bad-tempered hunchback working at tailoring or shoe repairing, with Victorian overtones. I am quite sure that these stereotypes seriously affect our attitudes and, as a result, our ways of helping and training handicapped people and that, however subconsciously, we are educating them to be the sorts of people that the general public expect and will accept. Obviously, a handicapped person with a sunny and gracious personality is going to be very much more popular and acceptable than one who has a serious chip on his shoulder and is difficult and boorish, but it seems very important that we should recognise that handicapped adolescents must have the same opportunities as other adolescents of going through the changeable, awkward, rebellious stages if they are to develop into mature adults and to be liberated fully from their parents. And how difficult it is to be rebellious and to opt out, if in fact you are physically dependent on other people for your most personal needs. I should imagine that most teenagers have at one stage or another flounced out of the room, banging the front door behind them and telling their parents that they are going to leave home for good. If you are handicapped, however, you may not be able to shout at your parents or reach the door on your own; you may not be able to bang it behind you and you certainly could not survive by yourself. How then, do boys and girls like this begin to exert their own personalities in the face of so much dependence on other people?

In this paper we have been looking at the attitudes of, and towards, disabled people in general and not in any particular setting. It is easy enough to say that if only the schools or training centres had done a better job, a particular disabled young man or woman might have been able to mix and integrate more effectively. Or if more disabled children attended comprehensive schools and were seen in the community other children would accept them better, and when they, in turn, became adults they would have more understanding of the whole situation of handicapped people. Obviously, both these comments are relevant, but I think the problems go much deeper than this. People with serious and obvious disabilities and impairments arouse many very real and conflicting emotions in other people, emotions which I am convinced are proper emotions, which should not be unthinkingly denied or suppressed. They are often quite appropriate responses to a situation which is distressing and painful and may arouse feelings of real sorrow, sympathy or embarrassment. What matters is the positive reaction to these conflicting emotions and it is here that those of us who are closely connected with disabled people should have most to offer to those who are not so personally involved, by helping them to understand and cope with the confrontation.

As a final point, I would like to question whether it is really appropriate to work towards social integration for everyone. Are there some seriously handicapped people whom we should try to protect from society? Can this 'putting away' ever be considered as coming to terms with the situation and facing reality?

To end on a more positive note, however, I would like to quote the words of an athetoid man, who in spite of having a severe speech defect, holds a responsible teaching position: 'Why do we want to be accepted like other people? Why not aim to be accepted as we are, which is different from other people?'

2

A research study on the integration of physically handicapped children in ordinary primary schools

Elizabeth Anderson

When I was invited to present a paper at this Study Group, I decided not to discuss any one aspect of integration in detail. Instead, I would like to outline what I consider to be the major aspects of the question and to say a little about each, using the findings of a research study which I carried out between 1969 and 1972.

This study was financed by the National Fund for Research into Crippling Diseases and my purpose was to study the integration of physically handicapped children of 'normal' intelligence (in effect from about IQ 75 upwards) in ordinary primary schools.

In this country ten categories of handicapped pupils are recognised. Educationally subnormal children comprise the largest category, followed by maladjusted children and then by the physically handicapped. A recent Department of Education and Science Survey suggested there are between 10,000 and 11,000 physically handicapped children in ordinary schools. About two-thirds of these are in primary schools. Approximately the same number of children were, in January 1971, receiving or awaiting special educational treatment in special schools. Within the special schools, cerebral palsy accounts for the largest group of children, followed by spina bifida, then by heart disease, muscular dystrophy, and congenital deformities of the limbs in that order. In ordinary schools children with limb deformities form the largest group, followed by those with heart diseases, the cerebral palsied, children with spina bifida and children with polio. Although the more severely handicapped children (particularly in the case of cerebral palsy) tend to be in the special schools, there is a considerable overlap as regards severity of handicap between physically handicapped children in ordinary and special schools.

The children in my own study included two groups. Their names were obtained from the handicapped registers of the Local Health Authorities. All were in ordinary schools. The first group consisted of seventy-four disabled children aged 7-11 in seventy-two different schools. About half were in London schools; the others were in town or village schools in five local authority areas outside London. Twenty-nine per cent of the children had congenital abnormalities of the limbs, 21 per cent cerebral palsy and 16 per cent spina bifida, usually with hydrocephalus. The others had a wide variety of physical handicaps. A more important way of characterising the children was in terms of whether they had purely physical handicaps (two-thirds of the group) or whether they had, in addition, neurological impairment (one-third of the group). Seventeen per cent of the children were mildly handicapped, 61 per cent moderately handicapped and 22 per cent severely handicapped.

I included a second group of children in the study made up of twenty-five children in infant classes (5-7 year olds); most of them suffered from cerebral palsy or from spina bifida and hydrocephalus, and most were severely handicapped.

These ninety-nine children were all in ordinary classes. In addition I visited all the special classes or units for physically handicapped children in primary schools in England which I could trace.

Elizabeth Anderson

Aims of the study

I singled out for attention four main aspects of integration:

First, I looked at the process by which the children came to be placed in ordinary schools. In particular I studied the attitudes of the parents to different types of schooling and the problems that they had encountered. I felt it very important to approach the problem from the consumer's point of view.

Second, I looked at the social and emotional adjustment of the children (including social relationships, social competence and the extent of emotional and behavioural disorders), especially in relation to their non-handicapped classmates.

Third, I looked at their academic attainments, again in relation to those of their non-handicapped peers.

Finally, I considered in detail the nature and the adequacy of the special provisions made for physically handicapped children in ordinary schools.

1 Placement problems

I needed to discover the views of the parents and teachers in my study on school placement. In my interview with the mother I asked either: 'How did you feel when special school placement was suggested for your child?' (since for well over half the children a special school had been seriously suggested, usually as an initial placement) or 'How would you have felt if this had been suggested?' Of the seventy-four mothers with junior school children, 4 per cent were in favour of special school placement, 13½ per cent uncommitted and the remainder opposed, often strongly. There was a similar pattern for the mothers of the more heavily handicapped infants. The main reasons for these attitudes were, first, the belief that the child would obtain a better education in an ordinary school and, second, the belief that he would benefit socially.

Although many local authority officials went to great pains to try to meet the parents' wishes, it was also the case that parents faced many problems connected with placement. These included the fact that advice about placement had come very late, if at all; that it was often inadequate or contradictory; that sometimes great persistence was needed before a child was recommended for an ordinary school and (although this was less of a problem) that ordinary schools had sometimes refused, or could not accept, disabled pupils.

I must also comment here on the views of the heads and class teachers. In the great majority of cases I found that, once a disabled child had been in an ordinary school for even quite a short time, their attitude was not simply one of acceptance but one of positive enthusiasm about the benefits of integration. Eighty-five per cent of the class teachers in the study thought that the present placement was the best one for the child; among the others several thought that a smaller class (but still in an ordinary school) would be preferable, while only 4.4 per cent thought that the child should be in a special school.

I shall have more to say about the teachers' viewpoints later in this paper, but I must emphasise here that I did find a most encouraging willingness among primary school teachers to accept responsibility for children who were in some way 'different'. At the same time, these teachers had received very little information or advice from anyone other than the parents on either the medical or the educational aspects of the children's handicaps.

2   Social and emotional adjustment

In studying the social and emotional adjustment of the children and their academic attainments I used, for the junior school children, a control group of 148 non-handicapped children. Each handicapped child had two 'controls', who were the two classmates of the same sex who were nearest in age.

The type of questions which we have to consider when physically handicapped children are placed in ordinary schools are these: Are the children happy there? Do they have real friendships with their classmates or do they tend to be isolated? Is teasing a problem? Do they find mixing a strain and do they show more emotional and behavioural disorders than their classmates? Does ordinary school placement encourage social independence?

I used a variety of well known tests and measures as well as interviews with the parents and teachers to explore these questions in considerable detail. I can only mention a few of the findings here.

The great majority of the children were undoubtedly happy at school. Although the results of sociometric testing showed that handicapped children as a group were chosen less often as friends than the controls, there were considerable differences according to the nature of the disability. Cerebral palsied children tended to be chosen less often as friends than other physically handicapped children (and this is in line with findings from other studies) whereas children with congenital abnormalities had almost as many friends as the controls. Neither severity of handicap nor incontinence were barriers to social acceptability. Overall 9 per cent of the handicapped children were 'isolates'; that is they received no friendship choices, compared to 3 per cent of the controls. The disabled children most 'at risk' of social isolation were those of below average ability and attainment level; they tended to come from either deprived or over-protected homes; three out of the seven were cerebral palsied, and all but one were boys.

Other aspects of social relationships considered included the extent to which the physically handicapped children were chosen in classroom group activities, the amount of contact they had with their classmates outside school, and the extent and nature of teasing. Findings in all these areas suggested that, from the social point of view, integration brings many more gains than losses. Teasing was only a minor problem: it was virtually confined to London schools, and generally took the form of name-calling. Staff were usually able to deal with it effectively. On the credit side, about half of the handicapped children (compared to two-thirds of the controls) saw their school-friends 'frequently' after school and at weekends and the amount of visiting between homes was comparable. Most parents were satisfied with the amount and quality of contacts that their children had with neighbourhood friends, and the children's scores on the Manchester Scales of Social Adaptation suggested that, with the exception of some of the neurologically abnormal group, the children were as independent as their handicaps allowed.

When the extent and nature of behavioural and emotional disorders were examined (measures including parent and teacher interviews and the Rutter-Graham Scales) a similar picture emerged. The children with purely physical handicaps appeared, at least at this age, to be coping well, emotionally, with ordinary school placement. On the teacher scales, for example, they showed a lower rate of deviant behaviour (9 per cent) than did the controls (19 per cent). On the other hand the neurologically abnormal children showed a higher rate of disorders, one in four being rated as 'deviant' on the teacher scale, and I think that these are clearly the children most 'at risk' in ordinary school. Another striking finding was that 88 per cent of the neurologically abnormal children were rated as having a short concentration span, compared to only 43 per cent of the other handicapped children and 35 per cent of the control group.

3 Academic attainments

Once again, my point is that we cannot consider physically handicapped children as a group but must distinguish between those with and without neurological abnormalities. In reading ability (measured by the Neale Test) the children without neurological impairment were similar in their attainments (both on accuracy and on comprehension) to their non-handicapped classmates. In number work ability, although they were a little poorer, there were no significant differences.

The neurologically handicapped children in comparison had much lower attainments. While the other children in the study were, on average, reading at an accuracy level a month below their chronological age, the neurologically impaired children were on average fifteen months below. In arithmetic, whereas 30 per cent of the other children were of 'below average' ability on a five-point scale, nearly four in five of the neurologically impaired group were below average.

These findings can, at least to some extent, be explained by the fact that the mean IQ (on a non-verbal intelligence test, NFER Non-Verbal 5) of the children with neurological impairments was only 83.8 (compared to 102 and 104 in the orthopaedically handicapped and control groups respectively). Nevertheless, the fact remains that a large proportion of neurologically impaired children are likely to need extra help in reading and even more so in number work and many are likely to have specific learning disabilities. Although most of those in the study were coping, often within a group of non-handicapped children of a roughly similar level, a great many of them (and of course many non-handicapped children) clearly needed but were not getting extra specialised help. I think such help could be provided within an ordinary school setting but that it has not yet been tackled in a very determined way. Until it is a barrier will remain in the integration of many children, however satisfactory the physical provision for them is in ordinary schools.

4   The nature and adequacy of special provision in ordinary schools

I wish to consider this from two points of view. First, what are the different areas in which special provision will be needed? Second, what are the different ways in which special educational treatment in ordinary schools can be organised?

1   The main areas in which special arrangements will be required can be listed under five main headings:
   1   special needs as regards transport, modifications to school buildings and furniture, and the provision of special equipment;
   2   personal assistance;
   3   the needs for therapy;
   4   the need for information and advice to members of the school community, including the other children, in some cases their parents, and finally all the staff, especially the class teacher;
   5   the need of some physically handicapped children for special teaching help.
I hope that other contributors will go into these areas in more detail than I have space to do, but I will make a few comments about each on the basis of my own research study findings.

First, transport, buildings and equipment. Most local authorities will provide special transport (usually by taxi) when this is required and so this is not a major problem. As regards adaptations to buildings, I found that these were occasionally made before the child arrived, but usually afterwards on an ad hoc basis. In several cases I found adaptations were clearly needed but had never been requested. Outstanding requirements were for modifications related either to poor mobility (such as the provision of ramps) or to toileting problems. There was often an unrecognised need for toilet privacy. I found that few special educational aids were being used in ordinary schools. In some cases teachers were not aware that a need existed, or they did not know what aids were available, or how they could be obtained. In many cases it would be beneficial for a medical officer, adviser in special education or therapist to approach the school to see what modifications or aids could usefully be provided rather than waiting for a request to be made.

The second area concerns personal assistance. Several local authorities are now very successfully meeting the daily physical needs of quite severely handicapped children (for example incontinent children) by appointing full- or part-time personal assistants to the school. Such people are known variously as 'welfare assistants', 'helpers' and so on. Their duties differ from one school to another — in some cases, for instance, they may, under the guidance of the therapist, do daily exercises with the child or, at the class teacher's invitation and under her direction, may help in the handicapped child's class (or in other classes) on the teaching side. Almost all the teachers who worked with such assistants found their help quite essential. Unless two or more physically handicapped children share an assistant this form of provision will be expensive. There are other potential drawbacks, one being that an uninformed assistant may over-protect a child. However, if it is properly thought out the system is an excellent one.

The third area is the need for therapy. In my study 7 per cent of the children individually placed in ordinary schools needed speech therapy and 12 per cent needed physiotherapy. Facilities varied from one area to another, but speech therapists were in short supply generally. In the case of physiotherapy, sometimes a weekly session at the local hospital met the child's needs. On the whole, however, the situation was discouraging for a child who needs intensive physiotherapy, and liaison between the school and the therapist was often poor. I feel strongly that there is a need for a small research project to be set up to explore the most effective ways of providing physiotherapy to children in ordinary schools in both rural and urban areas.

The fourth area of need is for provision of information and advice about the disabled children to the members of the ordinary school community. I think it is often very important for the non-handicapped children (and sometimes their parents too) to be prepared in advance for the arrival of a handicapped child in the class. It must be remembered that the person most in need of information and advice about both medical and educational problems is the class-teacher. Unfortunately, at present class-teachers usually receive very inadequate support. Nearly half of the junior school class-teachers in my study had initial anxieties about coping with a disabled child, and one in every three was dissatisfied with the amount of information she had been given, especially on the medical side. Among the infant school teachers (who had more severely handicapped children to cope with) four in five were dissatisfied. The class-teachers rarely had any contact, either in person, by letter or telephone, with the medical officer who had recommended the placement or the school medical officer. There is no doubt that, especially in the early stages and at regular intervals afterwards, such contact would be warmly welcomed.

Similarly little advice was available on the educational side. A wide range of problems may arise, and the extension of a system of advisers for special education with specific responsibility for children in ordinary schools is undoubtedly needed. At the same time, the colleges of education should be preparing teachers to cope with a wide variety of handicapping conditions in ordinary schools.

The fifth area of special need which I mentioned, that of arrangements for specialised teaching aid, particularly for children with specific learning difficulties, is really the other side of the same coin. Sometimes the difficulties of these children are undiagnosed. In other cases they are known to need special help but either the type or the amount of help available may be inadequate.

2   I have so far referred mainly to children placed individually in local schools, and have indicated that we must make a distinction between children with purely physical disorders — whose needs are often relatively easy to meet — and those whose neurological abnormalities give rise to additional learning difficulties. For the latter (and also for children with very severe physical handicaps) special arrangements are probably required, geared to the needs of a group of handicapped children rather than to individuals.

For many people the most obvious and perhaps the only form of group provision may appear to be the special class. In Scandinavia, for example, the special class system is increasingly being used as an alternative to the special school, particularly for children with severe physical handicaps, with specific learning disabilities in addition to a physical handicap, or with minimal cerebral dysfunction. We have very few such classes over here, and I think a strong case can be made for their extension. There are two provisos I must make. First, if special classes are to offer facilities equal in quality to those of special schools — and I see no reason why they should not do so — then comparable resources must be allocated to them. Second, it has to be remembered that if children are placed in special rather than ordinary classes, real integration is going to be much more difficult to achieve and will have to be carefully discussed and planned for by all the staff of the school.

For this reason I think that we must at least consider alternatives to the special class. An alternative which is already being experimented with is making extensive adaptations to a selected school, to appoint extra staff on the care side and to admit all 'suitable' physically handicapped children in the area who are then placed individually in ordinary classes. For some children this will be quite satisfactory; for those with special learning disorders it does not go far enough. The provision of special teaching help must be an integral part of the plan. One way of making such provision (while still keeping children in the ordinary classes for much of the time) is to set up a specially staffed 'help clinic' or 'resource room' in the school to which children can be withdrawn for as much specialised help as they need. Preferably, to ensure continuity if a teacher leaves, two specialist teachers should be appointed. They will spend part of their time teaching in the ordinary classes (and so keep up to date with current educational practice) and part in the 'clinic'.

Finally, let me conclude with two points which, I hope, sum up what I have been saying. The first is that, for any particular child, integration at school may be quite a complex matter which requires very careful planning. I need hardly say that in this planning, teachers in special schools have an absolutely essential contribution to make. Second, despite its complex nature, and the fact that for certain children (for example those with family problems), or at certain stages in a child's development, special school placement may be necessary, I am sure that many more children could and should be placed in ordinary schools under the different kinds of arrangements I have outlined here.

3
The future place of the handicapped in society

Jack Tizard

If we are to plan intelligently for the handicapped in society we have first to define our objectives, to set the goals that we wish to attain. The objectives must of course be in principle realisable in a definable social context, but they need not be tied too closely to the specific features of the immediate social and material environment. Well informed and imaginative planning has to take into account the rapid changes that are occurring in society. Moreover, it must explore to the full the implications of the truism that man, in a sense, makes his environment. Choices are open to us. The decisions that we make now actually determine the future and the choices that the future will offer.

All this is obvious enough. I wish here to sketch out a set of possible objectives for social policy as it affects the handicapped and to discuss their implications.

Ends and means

Let me first illustrate the interplay between ends and means by looking at another class of problem: that of planning a piece of research. Often the most useful service that a supervisor of a higher degree student can perform is to help him to clarify the problem that he is proposing to investigate. It is, in my experience, only the exceptional student who does not start worrying too early in his studies about the details of his projected investigation — the size of sample, the methods he will use to collect data, problems of data analysis and so on. Usually these worries loom large before the student is at all clear in his own mind about what it is that he is actually aiming to do. Naturally there are good reasons for the student's anxiety: he is conscious of his inadequacies as a potential investigator, and, more important, he does not want to waste a lot of time planning expeditions to the moon. There is, for example, no point at all in planning research which will necessitate the clinical study of numbers of children who suffer from diseases which occur only once in every million births, because such children are simply not available. So the student — and the supervisor — have always to keep in mind the feasibility of anything they plan.

However, one can easily be mesmerised by technology and once we get into the detailed problems of experimental design, computer programming and so on, the sheer complexity and interest of these issues has a way of taking over the research. What should be the servants of the investigator become his master. It is, I think, for this reason that much psychological and social research — and no doubt much research on the physical and biological sciences also — is so essentially trivial. However it might have started out, it soon gets so bogged down in technicalities that it ends up simply as an exercise designed to make use of a set of existing techniques, or a piece of apparatus available in the lab., in a slightly novel way. Such research usually makes no contribution whatsoever to knowledge: there is nothing in it that leads anyone to think differently about an issue from the way it was thought about before. Unless we keep our central objectives constantly in mind, we will inevitably fail to reach the goals that we originally set ourselves, and we will probably not reach any other worthwhile goal either.

When we turn from social science to matters of social policy we face a set of issues that are not dissimilar.

Professional planners are on the whole a very able set of men and women; but almost without exception they are too close to their problems and too pressed for time to be able to take a long-term view of wider objectives. In consequence, central, regional and local planning tends almost always to be concerned with ways of increasing and improving services modelled on well established lines. If the services do not seem to be working very well we try of course to find ways of adapting them. However, radical changes, fresh thinking and new approaches require more than this, and they usually have to start outside the system. The controversies over the planning of London illustrate this process very well. Given the enormous complexity and urgency of traffic problems, those responsible for the Greater London development plan were unable to rise above them. Critics have therefore argued that if London gets the roads the planners say it needs there will be nothing to see at the end of the journey. All that makes London worth living in will have been destroyed.

Goals set for the handicapped

The history of care and treatment of the handicapped also illustrates very clearly the inertia of central planning, and the manner in which ideology influences, and is itself influenced by, immediate practical planning constraints. A public policy for mentally and physically handicapped persons was first clearly enunciated during the latter half of the nineteenth century. It was based on two beliefs: first, that handicapped children could be educated to some extent if special provision was made for them outside the ordinary educational system, and second, that society had a moral obligation to provide asylum for those who could not live unaided inside ordinary society. These beliefs had negative as well as positive consequences. The positive consequences were that something was at last done as of right for handicapped persons who

24

before had received little or nothing outside the workhouse. The negative consequences were that the recipients of publicly provided special care and education were sharply marked off and segregated from the rest of society.

The nineteenth-century bases on which our present services rest do seem to me to be unacceptably narrow; and it is this narrowness which largely prevents us from planning truly comprehensive services for the future. The special educational treatment of individual children for example was in the past dependent upon their prior formal 'ascertainment' as 'handicapped'. Today 'assessment' has replaced formal ascertainment, but the assessment has not, at least until recently, for the most part been relevant to the remediation of the child's disabilities. It has instead been largely taken up with the elucidation of presumed aetiology, or with supposedly medical diagnosis. Again, the special services of today are very much off-shoots of the same thinking that led to the establishment of the first special services during an earlier age. Today we provide special services for more and more 'categories' of handicapped children, but most of the effort still goes on outside the ordinary class as the child is removed from his ordinary environment in order to receive special educational treatment. Hence the need for careful assessment — to ensure that he is a proper person to receive such treatment; hence too the lack of much in the way of special educational treatment for the large numbers of children who are not special enough to be removed from ordinary classrooms, even though they are not getting on at all well at school. We take children to specialists more often than we bring specialists to children (or to teachers).

The basis for a comprehensive service

If we were beginning today to plan social, educational and medical services from scratch, I think we would design them

25

very differently. We would start from different premises and we would reach rather different conclusions. It would not be the case that 30 per cent of our special school placements were in boarding schools; we would not today provide special schools for ten different 'categories' of handicapped children; special schools and special classes for the handicapped would not be so remote from ordinary education as many of them are today; much more attention would be paid to the diagnosis and treatment of children with mild, moderate or even severe handicaps within the ordinary school setting. We would, I think, start with community-based services; each local community providing education, medical and social services for all children irrespective of age or degree of handicap. It would not be the case that children who did not fit the local school would be sent somewhere else for education; instead all children would go to the same school, and the programme would be tailored for the special needs of individual children.

This would in a way be a return to more primitive concepts — the concepts of the village or the commune which accepts its members as they are, old or young, clever or dull, fleet of foot or lame. I do not wish for a moment to argue for a past in which such notions were fully practised — clearly this was not the case in the past or special services would not have been created — but I think the idea is right. I think that this is what parents and handicapped children themselves would like. It is what we would like for ourselves or our relatives; it is how most of us would wish it in the society of which we are members. As things are today, the very set-up of the services causes us to make too much of handicap. It is difficult to remain matter of fact about it all, to treat handicapped people naturally and to be accepted naturally as a person in return. The awkwardness of relationships comes out very clearly in the essays contributed by handicapped persons themselves to Paul Hunt's symposium published under the title *Stigma* (Geoffrey Chapman, 1966). One reason for this awkwardness is that we distance ourselves from handicapped persons by placing them in special settings alongside others whose disabilities resemble their own. We see little of children with severe handicaps and so they look rather odd to us, causing us to behave awkwardly when we meet them, and because they mix mainly with other handicapped persons, they in turn behave awkwardly to us.

The alternative approach I am advocating is the one which the Swedes call normalisation. Most people agree with it in principle, but many think it is starry eyed, unattainable 'at present', idealistic and so on. I do not agree with these criticisms. Inasmuch as a policy of normalisation is feasible (as it is, in that it is not based on claims that deny the facts of handicaps or imply that all handicaps can be cured) and inasmuch as we would like to see it come about, the problems of implementation become ones of operational research.

Today scientists and engineers are becoming increasingly more concerned with finding ways of achieving objectives which appear realisable in principle but which involve the invention of a technology which is not yet developed — space research is the standard example of this, but much research in medicine follows the same policy guidelines. The technical problems of integrating the handicapped in society seem tiny compared with those involved in getting men on the moon, but they loom large because we do not put the same effort into formulating them explicitly nor finding ways of solving them. I think that most of the technology required to do this is already available and that in attempting to apply it we would rapidly discover where the blocks lay and how to remove the most serious of them. The fact that in doing so we might require a higher proportion of the labour force to be employed in social services of all sorts is one of the strongest arguments for advocating such a policy. For today the proportion of the labour force required to undertake productive work is declining and we are increasingly faced with the disillusionment of young people and not-so-young people

Jack Tizard

who are unable to use their education and creative desires to work for the common good.

4
An exercise in integration

Pauline Skelly

I must first of all make clear the philosophy of life which
governed my approach to the way in which we organised
the task of integrating twelve Thalidomide children into
Dovecot County Primary School. I must admit that 'We did
it my way.' This does not mean that all my staff are tied to
acting in accordance with my instructions. In fact, they are
all free to follow their own bent and to use the approach
that best suits them. What we are all agreed upon as a staff
is rather an attitude to life and the goals that we wish to
reach. Since I had been head for some ten years before we
started on this particular project, it follows that the staff
that I had gathered around me tended to share my views
on what was of major importance and what was not.
Fortunately, it was also a very stable staff. This unity of
purpose is, I think, a vital prerequisite of any work which
depends more on attitudes of mind than on any other single
factor.

How did I come to believe that heavily handicapped
children should be educated in a normal school environment?
That view, I suppose, had been developing gradually throughout my teaching life. I had realised that each child was a
person exactly like me, coping with a difficult and frequently
incomprehensible world, creeping back into their shell exactly
like me when I am rebuffed, and expanding in the warmth
of sympathy and understanding. Bright or dim, introvert or

Pauline Skelly

extrovert, maimed or whole, they are people just like me.
Physical handicap makes it that much harder, but it is still
the same world into which they must fit; into which they
ardently desire to fit, inconspicuously and unremarkably,
like their fellows. Their reaction to being made to feel
different or special is the same as my reaction — distress,
anxiety, frustration and embarrassment. I believe fervently
that we are all entitled to feel ourselves accepted and
acceptable in the main stream of life.

I was first asked if I would be willing to attempt the integration of a group of Thalidomide children in the spring of
1968 on an experimental basis. (I was asked because of the
suitability of the one-storey building.) I was willing to do
this, but I rejected the word 'experimental'.

First, I discussed the idea with my staff and I found that
the entire staff were keen to be involved in the proposal. I
then felt that I could go ahead with the practical steps that
were necessary to turn the idea into reality. A medical
conference was held at Greenbank School of Rest and
Recovery which the children then attended and to which
they owed a great deal. The Medical Officer for Schools, the
Special Schools Adviser and the headmistress of Greenbank
attended and finally a list of twelve children was compiled.
There was some opposition to the idea that the most heavily
handicapped child should come to us, but I felt that only to
reject him would be to deal a cruel blow to one child and
that somehow we would manage to solve any problems that
he might present. In the event he has been very little trouble
and a most delightful member of our school.

In October 1968 we held a meeting for the parents of the
children already in the school. The Special Schools Adviser
addressed this meeting, at which nearly all our families were
represented, and he described the work that we proposed
to attempt. The meeting was then thrown open to discussion.
The parents were almost unanimous in their support for the
project. From this date onwards I wrote to the parents of the

children who were to join us and invited them to visit the school by appointment to see us at work; to see the surroundings that their children would be working in and the facilities that they would be offered, as well as to discuss with me any difficulties and anxieties which they might feel. All the parents accepted. They were unanimous in offering us their support.

I now felt that I had the prerequisites for success — that is, the support of all my staff and the support of all the parents concerned. The head of Greenbank very kindly allowed myself and some of my staff to visit her school on various occasions to get to know the children so that they would not feel that they were coming to complete strangers. My staff was also augmented by the appointment of two extra teachers. A new head of department post was created and a teacher with extensive experience in teaching at special schools was appointed to this. It was made clear at the time of the appointment that we were not setting up a 'special unit' within the school, but were integrating. This meant that her work would be with an 'integrated class'. A second appointment with a similar proviso was made. It is important that any staff from special schools who take part in this type of work should know what they are embarking on and should be willing to adapt to the new requirements. Our new head of department started working with the children in January 1969, at the Greenbank School. She returned monthly to Dovecot to discuss her work, the needs of the children and the various provisions that we would need to make. She spent the last fortnight of the spring term at Dovecot preparing for the children's arrival in the April. The children, therefore, already regarded one of our teachers as their teacher. They also knew some of us from our visits to Greenbank and the second extra teacher as she had spent her half-term holiday working with them. They also had their own welfare worker who had started working with them at Greenbank some time before the transfer. (The welfare

worker's duties are too diversified to be described here, but
they are vital to the success of such a project.)

Our own children had been prepared to receive the incom-
ing pupils with friendliness, kindness and consideration by
means of talks in assembly and discussions in the classroom,
and they were all ready and anxious to play their part. We
had warned them not to smother the newcomers in an
attempt to 'mother' them.

On the material side, two classrooms had been decorated
and suitable furniture and equipment provided. A room had
been prepared as a welfare room and a head teacher's
toilet had been modified and altered to suit their requirements. (As we had taken over buildings originally designed as
a secondary modern school, we were fortunately not short of
space.)

23 April 1969 was the great day. We had thought and
planned carefully; now we had to see how it worked in
practice. The new pupils arrived in two taxis and a minibus,
as they came from all over the Merseyside area. Time of
arrival 8.50 a.m.; time of leaving 4.00 p.m. This meant that
they experienced normal school hours for the first time in
their lives. The day must have seemed very long at first, but
they were all game. They initially worked in one group with
the same teacher who they had worked with since the
January. The other new teacher assisted while they all
became acquainted, which they did quickly. The group fell
naturally into two sections, a younger and older section.
Within two days they had separated into their own neighbouring rooms. Over the second half of the term the groups in
these classrooms were gradually extended into about twenty
children in the same age group. This helped to prepare them
for complete integration.

They joined the whole school for assembly on Friday 25
April, by which time they had already made many friends
in the school. For the first fortnight they played in the
enclosed garden areas with groups of children from the

corresponding age groups. They were allowed freedom during playtime and dinner periods to explore the school. They did this most thoroughly with their attendant friends, who by common consent came from the whole seven-plus to eleven-plus age range. For the first month they dined in their own classrooms. After these initial periods they graduated to playing in the main play areas and dining in the main canteen with 260 other children.

They attempted the same summer examinations as all other classes, after which I was able to allocate them to their appropriate classes. In July, together with six fourth-year children, they acted as hosts and hostesses to the visiting top class infants. They entertained them to biscuits and orangeade on the lawn whilst I talked to the mothers of the new intake in the assembly hall. They were by now old hands, showing the new-comers over their school.

I must emphasise that the children, both handicapped and whole, integrated spontaneously and happily. None of the difficulties we had anxiously foreseen and planned for arose. Another unlooked-for value of the work gradually presented itself. It was not only the handicapped child who benefited: the whole atmosphere of the school underwent a subtle change. Always friendly and helpful, although from a tough working-class district, the children developed an added awareness of each others' needs. That is not to say that the 'toughies' became less tough, but rather that they did show previously unknown qualities of compassion and understanding. This was not sentimental but direct and sensible. This in turn altered their relationships with staff and the staff's relationship with them. The non-handicapped gained as much as the handicapped from the exercise.

Medically, the Thalidomide children have been no trouble. A special schools nurse visited once a fortnight originally, but now only comes if she is specifically asked. They are seen by the school nurse and doctor in the normal course of their inspections. The only special need is for water in the classrooms. The attendance record of these children is very good.

To conclude, reports by educational psychologists agree that the children have developed both maturity and balance and now mix completely and unselfconsciously. Three who were withdrawn have emerged from their shells and become friendly and communicative. They cope with all school situations exactly as the non-handicapped children do. Over the four years, four children have left and been accepted into their own local junior schools, and six have moved on normally with their classmates — five to the comprehensive school that we feed and one to a Roman Catholic secondary school in her own district. The remaining two will move on this July, one to his own area comprehensive school and one to our own area comprehensive.

I have talked to both parents and children to try to find areas of criticism on where we might have done better or used different methods. There should, in theory, have been many such areas, but a précis of the parents' comments includes such statements as: school is his or her life; has loved every minute of it; bored on holidays; we have seen him develop rapidly into a normal boy and educational standards have improved tremendously. The children's comments include: I feel real here; I feel grown up; we have lots of fun; I don't feel a baby any more; we do real school-work and I have got on well.

T— when he left the school for the last time before going on to a comprehensive school lay down in the main entrance corridor and patted the ground over and over again, saying 'God bless Grant Road School.' This sort of appreciation is, of course, very heart-warming, but I have frequently felt distress that any group of parents and children should have been pushed by society to the point where they have to feel such overwhelming gratitude for what the rest of us regard as a right, namely the chance to join in normal life. Over the four years all the children have learnt a valuable lesson.

To look different is not important; they know that J— or K—, D— or G—, M— or T— are people with exactly the same ideas and aspirations as themselves.

Personally, I see one weakness in the scheme as we have operated it. The children have been brought out of their own residential area and therefore cut off in part from the child activities and friendships of their own district. Friendships formed in school can only on rare occasions be extended into out of school hours because of the journeys involved. I feel that ideally each child should be integrated into his own area school to avoid this isolation from home friendships.

For the last three and a half years the phrase 'Thalidomide Unit' as applied from the outside has been a source of amusement to us. We have never had a 'Unit' as there are no conscious differences. We just have 430 children growing up together in one normal junior school.

5

Designing for physically handicapped children – are you on the right level, Mr Architect?

Brian Goldsmith

This question implies a criticism of the architect. It must be realised, however, that there is very little information on this subject for the architect. My paper therefore is the result of research undertaken to examine and ascertain the criteria required to assist in the design of schools for physically handicapped children.

Kershaw adequately describes the handicapped child — 'the motor, sensory, emotional or intellectual impairment of the handicapped person is something which holds him back in competition with ordinary people'. There is, of course, no 'handicap' when a physically handicapped child is in the company of physically handicapped children: the impediment comes when competing with 'whole' children. Much more mental and physical effort is expended to achieve the same results as a normal child, probably taking twice as long and usually requiring supervision.

The physically handicapped child must work within his capabilities, both mental and physical, which infers a restricted range of activity when compared with an ordinary child. For example the spina bifida child not only experiences the difficulty of moving about on paralysed legs but also, due to incontinence, can experience social embarrassment if far from a toilet. In strange surroundings the blind or deaf child will feel completely lost.

There does exist a school of opinion that considers that

few concessions should be made for a physically handicapped child, implying that he must be trained and educated in preparation to live and work in our society with normal people. In theory there is much to advocate such a philosophy; in practice it is impossible. The degree of handicap will decide if the former theory is to be adopted, but for a severely handicapped child, such as one who attends a school for physically handicapped children, concessions must be made. Mentally he must be taught within his capability, at his own pace for learning, and physically his environment must be modified and adapted to encourage maximum activity.

There are basic conditions of handicap to be considered. Children may be mentally normal or abnormal, wheelchair-bound or ambulant. In turn they may be dependent on or independent of supervision. Each of these conditions produce their own functional requirements in a building complex. In short, 'physically handicapped children are those who on account of physical and mental impairment are handicapped in their use of conventionally designed buildings, because of the lack of suitable facilities' (Selwyn Goldsmith, *Designing for the Disabled*, Royal Institute of British Architects, 1967).

Following the Education Act of 1944, all local authorities prepared and submitted to the minister their development plans, which included facilities for the 'special education' of physically handicapped children. These plans included the reassessment of existing school buildings and their suitability for educational purposes, especially for handicapped children.

From observations made by medical experts and educationalists, it is apparent that retarded and emotionally disturbed children make better progress in special schools, whereas previously they 'roughed it' in normal day school. A constant review of conditions is required to meet the requirements of the varying handicaps.

Generally the syllabus for both day and boarding schools is arranged to give pupils, as far as their handicap allows, a basic education similar to ordinary schools. Such a syllabus

includes sports and games, swimming, visits to places of
interest as well as cultural activities. A major item in a pupil's
syllabus is treatment for his particular handicap. This treatment forms a real part of school life and is always done under
expert supervision. In this respect aids are provided for
partially deaf and blind and physically handicapped pupils. It
is always the aim of the schools to rehabilitate their pupils in
ordinary schools.

The need for special boarding schools continues with the
increased incidence of severe handicaps and mental maladjust-
ments, both of which require specialised and constant care
beyond that which parents are usually able to give.

The design of schools for the physically handicapped child
is the subject of this paper. These are children who are
physically handicapped by disease or crippling defect and
who cannot be educated and cared for in an ordinary school.
Basically the children fall into two groups — ambulant and
wheelchair-bound, both of which produce their individual
problems for the architect. For instance, under the
'Handicapped Pupils and Special Schools: regulations', the
maximum number in a class is twenty but this is invariably
reduced according to the total severity of handicap: twenty
wheelchair cases would be impossible to manage in one
classroom. Some children are completely immobile and yet
possess average intelligence which causes enormous frustration. In these circumstances the environment is of paramount
importance to assist them with their physical disability and
to reduce their sense of frustration. Outdoor activities,
individually and collectively, are encouraged for all handicaps.
These activities make the most of local amenities, such as
swimming baths, parks and museums, etc.

'The environment should be peaceful, orderly and predictable with the adults being firm, confident and supporting',
wrote Dr Mary Wilson in her booklet *The Education of
Brain Injured Children in the United States of America.*
Physically handicapped and maladjusted children require the

support of an environment where the physical and emotional components are completely integrated and assist in promoting relationships with others. To achieve this object the school should be designed to allow for the simultaneous and flexible use of facilities by individual children or groups of children at the varying stages of adjustment. The segregation applies to the layout of teaching areas, more than to separate 'family groups' suggested by the appointment of a substitute mother and father (housematron) in present day special schools.

Within the context of this paper, environment refers to the school's physical environment which contributes to the psychological needs and well-being of the children. This consideration is basically a planning issue — determining the relationship of functional areas for ease of use and satisfying the complex facets of human nature. The emphasis is on the psychological needs, as well as the physical. It is necessary to consider all design aspects from the viewpoint of the wheel-chair child who has to propel himself, sometimes unaided, through all areas. Are the doors wide enough to avoid scraping the knuckles? Can the door be easily opened again in order to leave the room? These questions, and many others, confront a physically handicapped child; therefore adequate provision must be made to give the wheelchair child confidence, before education proper can begin. This situation is described by Himes in *Schools Environment Research Report 1956:* 'The planning of spatial relationships . . . is now largely based on the use of a variety of modules related to the dimensional requirements of the activities alone.' Space as a component of environment has become an organisation of these quantitative modules. It is almost impossible to obtain a child's reaction to a particular environment or to evolve an environment that will be suitable to the child's needs. Anthropometric data can be physically measured, but environmental data can only be determined individually for each child by a series of tests which may provide unreliable results.

Brian Goldsmith

It is generally considered that environment contributes to the character of a person, but the influence of human beings occupying the environment cannot be underestimated. It is likely that a child brought up among criminals would be affected in some way, regardless of the environment. On the other hand, a well dispositioned child brought up in a united and happy family will feel the environment to be correct because the atmosphere is one of security. Although designers may strive to produce what they consider to be good environments, it will be the teaching staff who will eventually create the atmosphere and so improve or destroy the intended environment of the school. In line with this observation some authorities consider the building to be of no importance, the teaching staff providing the required atmosphere. Such a concept is unacceptable here because all human beings have the ability of choice and are educated to have preferences, therefore one environment would be preferred to another and so on, within our whole environment. Simple tests of subjecting people to different experiences and then measuring their reactions are well known for determining a suitable environment for that person.

One important environmental factor emerges in designing schools, and that is scale: scale related to children, particularly the wheelchair cases, who observe the world from about 3 feet 8 inches above floor level. Although perception changes as a result of education and maturity, the environment of a school should be designed for the child, especially in the primary nursery accommodation where the child should be the measure of all things.

To summarise the subject of environment, the following was reported by Kahan in 1965:

The problem is how to design a physical space with its visual elements which serves a purpose for each and every person using it, and at the same time reflects and enhances the most desirable aesthetic experience expressing this purpose (Kenneth Bayes, *The Therapeutic Effect of Environment on Emotionally Disturbed or Mentally Subnormal Children*, Kangman, International Design Award Study, 1964-6).

In a wheelchair a man's height is decreased by one third and his width is doubled. His reach is limited by his inability to get his body into close proximity with objects because of the way the wheelchair is constructed. He needs more room to carry out normal everyday activities. He cannot climb steps. He can go forward and backward at will, but cannot move abruptly to either side. To travel in a straight line he needs a path 3'0" wide, and he needs almost 5'0" of straight travel before he can negotiate a turn. 27 sq.ft. of clear area is needed to permit him to turn about. This is the new entity to be considered when identifying and solving exterior and interior design problems (*Making Facilities Accessible to the Physically Handicapped*, State University Construction Fund, Albany, New York, July 1967).

While it is the constant intention to return the physically handicapped child to an ordinary school, the large majority never accede to this position. In the school for physically handicapped children the sharp division between work and play adapted in ordinary schools has to be relaxed almost to the point of abolition in the primary classes, gradually re-establishing the ordinary school principle in the last years of schooling. The whole gamut of 'living and learning' as expressed in playing, schooling, eating, bathing or pottering about doing nothing is taken as a process in the child's education, because for some of the children the difference between 'living and learning' does not exist or perhaps exists only for very short periods of time. Added to this the remedial and therapeutic function of the school, combined with possible medical treatment, suggests that 'living and learning' should be considered as one overall activity without physical division in the teaching areas except in the senior classes. It is considered by some authorities that the casual atmosphere of an open-planned environment, maintaining constant contact with adults, can be of crucial importance to the child's development.

The concept of my philosophy is based upon the following principles which will improve the standards of education in relation to the present circumstances of teacher/pupil ratio:

1   Admission, nursery and residential 2-5 years. Basically child care units segregated from the remainder of the school; open-plan with playroom interior complete and sand and water pits in the admission classrooms.
2   Primary 5-7 years. An open-planned area as an extension of the home environment, using furniture and fittings to define activity areas, including residential pupils; designed to reduce the break between home and school, which is very disturbing to maladjusted children, and to assist staff supervision especially in group activities.
3   Junior 7-11 years. A transitional stage between primary and secondary grading where the home environment is reduced and semi-permanent cellular planning is introduced with the use of sliding partitions, maintaining maximum flexibility for individual or group tuition.
4   Secondary 11-16 years. Permanently segregated classrooms with quiet or non-distractibility corner areas defined by removable furniture and fittings with the environment designed as an introduction to the office and workshops atmosphere.

The admission, nursery and primary areas would be thoroughly designed, with special physical aids for therapeutic training included in the education curriculum. In the junior areas the special physical aids will be reduced and everyday fittings and fixtures introduced. For the secondary areas there would only be the essential special physical aids for the incurable children (based on the standards of the Code of Practice No. 96 prescribed for public buildings). Although it is argued that usually no provision is made in the child's home, it must be remembered that in a house there is considerably more furniture in a much smaller area, which in itself becomes a physical aid. Nevertheless, medical advice should be sought concerning the particular handicap to ascertain whether alterations to the home are necessary.

Thus, four basic environmental areas are involved, each evolving out of the other, until the child is 16 years old or more, if it is in the pupil's interests to stay on at school prior to vocational training. Each area should be individually designed to differentiate it from the others and to give the child a sense of progression through the school, both physically and emotionally. Such environmental areas will give the child a feeling of security as he develops socially, practically and intellectually. This does not imply that the four basic elements of the building are entirely different; on the contrary, the relationship between the various areas should be close, the association with these areas being deeper and developing upon familiarity. An integrated design enables the child to find a graduated range of experiences, each requiring greater involvement and more concentrated effort.

While it is necessary to design a school for physically handicapped children as an integrated 'whole', it is equally necessary to differentiate between the various areas enumerated earlier, making them initially recognisable, thereby reducing, or even eliminating, ambiguity. By adopting an 'open plan' it is possible to merge differing functional areas into one large area so that each area is integrated into the overall conception. However, the architectural treatment of each area must be easily recognisable, creating its own environment if possible. Even in dormitories bed spaces can be treated to reflect the personality of the individual child.

Some of the many factors which contribute to the easy

functioning of a school building are enumerated for reference:

1 All furniture to be standardised in design but with different colours identified with each area. This principle can be applied to doors, gates and built-in furniture.

2 Ironmongery to be standardised, especially the lock suiting, using a master key and sub-masters for different areas, but the door and window furniture being common to all areas.

3 Lighting and switching can be standardised in all areas occupied or used by children so that a child upon entering a room or area instinctively knows where to find the light switch. The same principle applies to socket outlets.

4 The use of glass must be carefully controlled, using safety glass throughout. Ordinary people have been known to walk through a fixed glass panel having mistaken it for a door. Similarly, glazed partitions must be carefully detailed to avoid similar accidents. Door springs and 'bomber' hinges are not advocated because of the vicious swing that can result from their use. Secret doors must never be used as they are difficult to locate, especially in an emergency.

5 Sanitary ware must be robust, self-cleansing and simple in design, with fittings designed for hospital-type usage; fittings must be placed at lower levels for wheelchair and semi-ambulant users. Similarly, mirrors and shelves must be within easy reach to avoid accidents.

6 'Jazzy' interiors cannot be contemplated as children with visual perception difficulties can become confused and even frightened. For example, exaggerated perspective, continuing vistas in long corridors or mirror reflection giving a sense of infinity should be avoided. Heavily grained timber or patterned ceilings are equally disturbing. Deep structural cantilevers are known to be disturbing because they appear to be falling down, and therefore produce a built-in threat.

7 If a heating system of low pressure hot water with radiators is adopted, it is important that all radiators are protected or positioned to prevent a paralysed limb in contact with the radiator becoming, unknowingly, burnt.

Hot water fittings or pipes should be similarly protected. All
hot water to sanitary fittings should pass through a mixer to
a predetermined temperature to avoid accidents by scalding.

8   Guard rails, grip handles, hand rails, chair rails and barriers
are to be used as necessary. Their function is to assist the child
in overcoming the deficiency of his physical handicap, not to
make him feel abnormal.

9   The floor covering and finish to be free from any obstruction that could cause accidents. For example, children in
calipers drag their feet; this could cause a fall if a threshold
floor tile or manhole frame rim projected above the general
level of floor. All finishes must be smooth, yet unpolished,
to avoid slipping, especially on ramps between two different
floor levels. Ribbed rubber or neoprene is excellent for
gradients where ambulant and wheelchair cases are not under
constant supervision.

10   Walls should be finished in hard-wearing material easily
cleaned or replaced if necessary. Even if a hand rail is provided,
dirty finger marks are an everyday occurrence for children
seeking support or reassurance from a wall. If hand rails are
provided they should be continuous even across door openings,
where they can be fixed to the door as a grip rail.

11   Up to now stairs have been disliked in schools for handicapped children, but for therapeutic reasons there is a case
for their inclusion in secondary routes. Stairs should not occur
on main fire escape routes in case a quick exit is necessary.

12   Externally, the principle of flat, smooth surfaces is
continued with adequate rail barriers provided at change of
level as necessary. Play areas with raised planting beds and
grass lawns are encouraged to promote an interest in gardening activities. Wheelchair races are a common sport in playtime, especially with battery operated models. As these races
could lead to accidents, long stretches of paving are to be
avoided, especially if ramps or gradients are contained within
the length of paving.

13   The problem of fire and general emergency exits from

all parts of a school building creates real difficulties for the architect, especially when considering the restricted mobility of physically handicapped children. The corridors are wider than for normal children, to facilitate wheelchair traffic, and fire escape doors are fitted with simple lever handles, operated from inside the building, which throw the bolt when locked from outside. The school must be clearly signposted to indicate the route and method of escape. A fire alarm installation must be designed to operate bells throughout the school and not just at the location of the fire. Extra fire-fighting equipment must be sited at strategic points and must be easily accessible. It is advantageous to provide an escape door to the outside in every classroom so as not to rely upon arduous escape routes, which could act as funnels for smoke. A spiral slide or straight chute replaces the fire escape stair-case from upper floors.

Much has been written on the subject of colour and its effect on maladjusted children at varying stages of their scholastic life. From investigation one fact emerges: children enjoy big areas of bright colour. However, in the younger age groups they do not seem to react emotionally to colour stimulus. The maximum stimulation comes from their own pictures and the colours contained in them. Building colours tend to disturb the staff more than the children. As a maximum amount of pin-up boarding should be provided, the colours of classrooms should be in a low key in contrast to the vibrant coloured pictures of the children. Identification of functional areas by the use of colour has proved successful. This can be achieved by the colour coding of doors and panels, floor materials, wall finishes or furniture and fittings. Picture or colour symbols are used extensively in classes for identifying personal belongings. This is especially important for the child who cannot read. The results of tests carried out on the reactions to colours are varied, but it has been proven with maladjusted children that primary colours stimulate and dark colours depress.

With the ever-increasing problem of noise from traffic and aeroplanes, it is becoming necessary to insulate against such noises as they contribute towards distractions in class. This raises a problem with space frame and infill panel construction, as the insulation properties for noise are not so good as with traditional forms of construction which have weight and density. Controlling noise at its source also helps to reduce distractions and the acoustic treatment of classrooms, corridors and noisy activity areas is essential, especially in open plans. A short reverberation time in teaching areas is ideal, especially with partially hearing children, who rely upon clear sound and diction for ease of comprehension.

This paper on designing for physically handicapped children would not be complete without a mention being made of the physical aids, equipment and furniture used in this type of school. The personal aids of a child need not be analysed i.e. crutches, walking frames, wheelchairs, calipers, braces, etc. as they do not form a part of the building. The basic function of physical aids is to help a physically handicapped child help himself. Before an aid or piece of equipment is selected, the following points should be considered:

1 is the activity within the limit of feasibility?
2 determine need and interest,
3 age and occupational use,
4 availability or alternative,
5 selection of materials for their inconspicuousness, indestructibility, cleanliness, weight, handleability and expense,
6 maintenance: from a research on materials the following have proved most suitable — aluminium, plastics, melamines, pine, oak and ply woods, chromium plated steel, calf or horse-hide leather.

The majority of children, either wheelchair-bound or ambulatory, have only partial use of limbs or body. It is impossible to design every facet of a building to suit the diversity of all the children's handicaps; therefore average dimensions are used, leaving the furniture used by individual children to be adapted to suit their handicaps. These alterations are carried out in the school by the school carpenter, senior therapist and possibly the head. The child's actions and capabilities are analysed, his working limbs measured and a 'mock-up' piece of furniture made. These actions usually involve taking a piece of standard furniture and adapting it to suit the dimensions taken earlier. The child is then given the article and is observed over a period of time to ascertain if any refinements are required or alterations necessary. After a satisfactory testing period the piece of furniture is made into a 'permanent special' and the user's name placed on it, and the relevant data filed for future reference. If the handicap is permanent and not likely to improve then the child will use the article throughout his school life, altering it if necessary. When the child leaves the school the article must be stored until another child with similar handicaps joins the school, when the article can be re-used. The furniture most affected includes toilet seats or frames, feeding chairs, classroom/playroom desks/ tables and chairs, beds and accessories to wheelchairs.

The problems of designing for physically handicapped children have been defined and analysed in an attempt to assess the criteria required to evolve a correct environment for educating these children. The ergonomics of an environment comprising their human needs, perception, reactions, sensations of space, physiological comfort, social relationships and the use of the mental faculties must be constantly borne in mind when trying to interpret these abstractions into such material concepts as buildings for physically handicapped children. It is therefore essential that the architect should not work in isolation but in collaboration with psychiatrists, psychologists, therapists, sociologists, doctors and educationalists.

Am I on the right level?

6

The problem of the
multiple - handicapped child

James Loring

In this paper I will try to throw some light on the suitability
of ordinary schools for the education of moderately or
severely handicapped children. In doing so I shall draw
directly from the experience of the Spastics Society in this
field and also from my own experience of our schools and
centres.

The background information to this problem is that in
January 1971 there were approximately 117,000 pupils in
England and Wales being provided with special education
and approximately 6,000 awaiting admission for more than
one year. Of the 117,000 pupils, 68,000 were deemed to be
educationally subnormal, 15,000 maladjusted, 12,000
physically handicapped, 8,000 delicate children and the
remaining numbers were spread between blind, partially
sighted, deaf, partially hearing, epileptic and speech defect.
Throughout all categories there were more boys than girls.
There were 7,817 teachers or full-time equivalent of part-
time teachers. There are, therefore, very substantial numbers
of children receiving special education and the resources tied
up in this field are considerable, both in human and financial
terms.

Large numbers of handicapped children are educated in
ordinary schools but there are no comprehensive statistics.
However, there is information about handicapped children in

special classes. In primary schools handicapped children in special classes amount to 8,287 full-time pupils and fifty-four part-time pupils. We also know that there are 1,590 handicapped pupils in special classes in secondary schools. The falling-off from approximately 8,000 in primary schools to 1,590 in secondary schools is quite interesting and probably significant. Presumably the majority of handicapped children who can be educated and managed in primary schools cannot be suitably dealt with after the age of 11 in secondary schools.

There is remarkably little information about the way in which these children progress and the problems which they present. There is a strong social movement in this country and elsewhere towards comprehensive education. This has been confined until relatively recently to the proposition that children of different social backgrounds and intelligence levels benefit from being educated together. The advocates of comprehensive education pay special attention to the social advantages of such a mixture and rather less to the educational advantages in the narrow sense of the word. It has now become commonplace to advocate extending the intelligence ranges to include children with at least some measure of mental handicap and furthermore to advocate the inclusion of children with a severe physical handicap in the ordinary education system. However, whether children who were recently transferred from local health authorities to local education authorities can benefit from ordinary, as distinct from special education, has yet to be evaluated. There are important indications that they can benefit but it is very doubtful indeed whether the majority of teachers without special training have either the temperament, the ability or the experience to help these children. The transfer of these children to special classes in ordinary schools without effective re-training of teaching staff would produce very few helpful results.

Special education in this country has a long history and one of achievement. In 1870 statutory authorities began their task of educating ordinary children and within a few years of compulsory education the London School Board had passed their first resolution about blind and deaf children. The earliest public provision of special education was for children handicapped by blindness or deafness. The Elementary Education (Blind and Deaf Children) Act of 1893 laid down the duty of the school authority to make special provision for those pupils. At this time the minimum school leaving age for ordinary pupils was 11 years but the Act gave power to enforce compulsory attendance of blind and deaf pupils up to the age of 16. There were further enactments over the years which brought other handicaps within the scope of the Education Acts. Special education was brought into existence because of the inability of ordinary schools to educate handicapped children, and it could be argued that for a large number of handicapped children education only became a possibility with the creation of special schools.

It is therefore important that before we launch an attack upon the so-called segregation of handicapped pupils in special schools it should be understood that their transfer to ordinary schools would be an operation of considerable complexity and would be considered by some to be a retrograde step. The principal administrative categories are blindness and partial sight, deafness and partial hearing, educational subnormality, epileptic, maladjusted, physically handicapped, speech defect and delicate. The transfer of some of these children to some ordinary schools might at the moment mean that they would, unless special arrangements were made, sink into the D and E streams. The more severely handicapped children require special facilities and these do not exist in many schools. The admission of the physically handicapped in particular will require quite substantial alteration to present buildings. A great many ordinary schools are themselves sub-standard, particularly those in educational priority areas. A great many of the new schools are not designed to take handicapped pupils.

James Loring

In order to come to grips with the problem I think one should state that the major consideration·is that a child should be educated in a school and in circumstances which are most appropriate to the child's ability and function. It would, in my opinion, be improper, even cruel, if handicapped pupils were transferred from special schools, many of which have a higher standard than ordinary schools, to schools which are not organised or designed to contain them and may be functioning at an inferior level, simply to satisfy doctrinaire educational theory. One of the problems is that there is very little research evidence about the relative progress made by handicapped children in ordinary schools. This is not a concealed attack on the education of handicapped children in ordinary schools, but rather a plea that the child's interest should always be put first and that the primary object of schooling is education, not social engineering.

Cerebral palsy does not appear as a separate administrative category and the majority of educable cerebral palsied children who are receiving special education are included in either the physically handicapped or educationally subnormal categories, although they could feature in any one of the other categories if that category defined the child's major presenting handicap.

A large number of cerebral palsied children are educated in ordinary schools or local authority special schools. The Spastics Society generally speaking educates children for whom there are no suitable local education facilities (see Table 6.1). In 1965 I undertook a survey of children in six of our boarding schools in which at that time there were 315 pupils. The information is contained in the book *Teaching the Cerebral Palsied Child* (Spastics Society/Heinemann, 1966), and it was revealed that in addition to the major presenting handicap, there were often secondary and tertiary disorders which averaged approximately two to three per pupil. More recently a survey has been undertaken of a large

Table 6.1   The Spastics Society's educational network

	No. of units	No. of pupils
Boarding schools administered by the Society	7	468
Further education centres administered by the Society	2	63
Schools affiliated to the Society	4	257
Education units administered by local groups of the Society		
(a) Providing nursery care and education	19	514*
(b) Providing nursery care only	7	111*
Total	39	1,413*

*Approximate figures

number of children (466) at our schools and a similar pattern
of additional disorder is revealed (see Table 6.2). The major
additional disorders which I categorised were:

1   significant speech defect;
2   significant hearing loss;
3   significant visual defect;
4   epilepsy;
5   spatial difficulties;
6   emotional disturbance.

These defects present substantial problems to teachers.

In addition to the seven schools that I have mentioned in
Table 6.2 the local groups of the Spastics Society provide
approximately twenty-nine centres for children. Children
attending these centres amounted to 700 in April 1970 and
that number has now been reduced by the closure of two
centres. Two others have been handed over to local authorities. The children were broadly categorised by Mr Mahoney,
the Society's Education Officer, and it was considered that
224 were educable, using the word in its broadest sense, 202
were severely subnormal and trainable and 272 were severely

Table 6.2 Survey of seven schools run by the Spastics Society

No. of children	School	Significant speech defect	Significant hearing loss	Significant visual defect	Epilepsy	Spatial difficulties	Emotional disturbance
80	Thomas Delarue	32	14	32	2	13	–
120	Meldreth Manor	50	13	27	37	36	7
25	Hawksworth Hall	20	6	3	5	9	5
56	Ingfield Manor	36	12	4	7	27	18
63	Irton Hall	40	9	21	12	31	17
65	Wilfred Pickles	40	14	4	3	28	31
57	Craig y Parc	31	7	8	12	18	8
466		249	75	99	78	162	86

subnormal with a gross handicap. The children ranged from
approximately 1 year to 16 years. These were children for
whom there was little or no local authority provision. No
doubt the enforcement of the Education (Handicapped
Children) Act 1970 will improve their situation. The great
majority of the children, apart from physical and mental
handicap, have a pattern of subsidiary handicaps not unlike
that in our ordinary schools, though in many cases the
handicap would be more severe. The pattern of additional
handicap in the seven schools surveyed (466 children) is as
follows:

1	significant speech defect	249
2	significant hearing loss	75
3	significant visual defect	99
4	epilepsy	78
5	spatial difficulties	162
6	emotional disturbance	86

although the latter is necessarily an arbitrary and tentative
figure.

I do not want to pontificate upon the general proposition
of integrating handicapped children in ordinary schools, but
if educational administrators seriously think that they can
easily integrate the 1,200 children that I have mentioned into
ordinary schools they are lacking in realism. They are, faute de
mieux, in our schools because other schools cannot take
them. No doubt the situation will be eased as the years go on,
but I appeal very strongly to all concerned to evaluate the
classroom problems which stem from children who have a
speech defect, a hearing loss or visual defect; problems which
from an educationalist's point of view are perhaps more
important than spatial difficulties and emotional disturbance.
I would ask them whether in their schools or schools under
their jurisdiction there are facilities for caring for, managing
and educating such children, and if not what are their plans
for providing these facilities. Is physiotherapy readily
available on the site? A high percentage have a significant

speech defect: is speech therapy available in the school? Are there facilities for teaching children with significant hearing loss and significant visual defect? Are the schools able to deal effectively with epileptic children? What specific learning difficulties are masked by these defects, in particular in those children with spatial difficulties? Approximately 50 per cent of the Society's children are in wheelchairs — will they be able to move freely about the school? These and other questions must be answered satisfactorily. Are there to be special classes in primary schools, using the primary school as an assessment situation? Are there to be special classes in secondary schools? What proportion do they see as being transferable to ordinary classes in ordinary schools, and most important of all, which do they really prefer — segregation in an ordinary school or integration in a special school?

Finally, I would like to make a reference to the parents. Parents of handicapped children for the most part will prefer that their children should be part of an ordinary school community and not unnaturally they would wish them to continue to be so for the remainder of their school life. This is a quite legitimate social aspiration. But are these views realistic, given the present standards of many primary and ordinary schools? It seems to me to be quite clear that each child's future must be considered individually. No doubt there will be some children who will be able to join ordinary classes in due course, but for many others transfer to existing all-age special schools or new special schools is the most that can be expected.

However, I would not like anything I have said to spoil the spirit of enterprise in teachers who are trying to include handicapped children in their classes. All things being equal I would prefer handicapped children to be cared for and educated in the main stream. My misgiving stems not from faulty philosophy in this matter, but rather from the certainty that ordinary schools have a very large number of problems to solve and that, for the most part, they are not yet ready to take handicapped children.

7
Preparing handicapped children for life

Anita Loring

In a highly competitive world where success is judged by achievement, economic status and very often conformity to a highly complex set of social attainments and values, the handicapped child has to learn not only to accept the limitations placed upon him by his handicap, but also how to measure up to all the demands which society places upon him. Very often his task is made even more difficult by the preconceived notions that society itself has of the handicapped, and the handicapped person then finds himself in a situation in society in which he has to prove himself in his own right as an ordinary human being. The business of learning is for most people a life-long occupation which begins the moment the child is born. Although the child learns much from his parents, he also spends many of the formative years of his life at school and therefore the obligation of preparing the child for adult life falls heavily not only upon the parents but upon the staff of the school which the child attends.

If one asks staff in the school what they see as the main purpose of education, the answer will often be that it is a preparation for life. In the research that I have been undertaking, I have tried to disentangle the more specific means which are used to prepare children for the outside world. I have in fact been trying to identify in school life those procedures, not associated with specific subject-teaching, which are used to acclimatise a child to the demands of adulthood.

The work was undertaken in four schools, a school for the blind, one for the deaf, a school for children with mixed handicaps and a school for the cerebral palsied. All the schools chosen were boarding schools containing both boys and girls of average intelligence. The project was confined to boarding schools since the inclusion of children going to day school would introduce many other factors into the situation and in England at least it is very often the residential schools which take the most severely handicapped children, and it is with this group of children that the greater problems seem to occur when they leave school.

The information for this work was gathered in two ways. First, the staff in the schools concerned who were willing were interviewed by means of a guided interview schedule and a tape recorder. Second, the children who were willing who had just recently left the four schools involved were sent a questionnaire which could be filled in by hand. The children were therefore of school leaving age ranging from 16 to 20 years. They had to be of average intelligence in order that they could actually understand the questions that they were being asked, and it was necessary to make the questionnaire as simple as possible, bearing in mind the very severe degree of handicap in some cases.

The questions to the staff were divided roughly into the following sections:
1   Belief and attitude about life in general.
2   Their attitude towards handicap.
3   How they viewed their role in the school.
4   Knowledge about school in general and what goes on in it.
5   Off duty role.
6   Specific situation questions.
7   A certain amount of background information.
8   Questions regarding the problems of sex and marriage for the handicapped.
The children's questionnaire asked approximately half the

same questions as those given to the staff, and the rest related in many ways to areas of similar interest.

I would like to emphasise that I have not checked any of the answers given to me to see if they are factually correct. For example, if I had been told by one group of people that a particular school owned six donkeys, and by another group that the same school had no donkeys at all, I did not spend my time touring the school concerned looking for donkeys! It is in fact the discrepancies in such factual information that I find particularly interesting.

There were very great differences in the amount of time taken for children to settle down in a new school. This ranged from one week to four years. The average time taken was five and a half months, roughly equal to two school terms. Those who had been to the school for the blind seem to have settled down the quickest, and in general, the younger the child went to the school concerned the shorter the time it took to settle down. None of the four schools organised specific activities to help new pupils settle in, and it would be interesting to know whether pupils would settle down more quickly if some types of social activity were organised especially for them.

An overwhelming number of this group of children have never been to a school for non-handicapped children. This is probably due to the fact that the children at these four schools are very severely handicapped, most having more than one handicapping condition. Most ordinary schools in England would not, at this moment in time, be able to cope with such severe degrees of handicap from a caring point of view nor are there sufficient numbers of specially trained teachers in these schools who could cope with the children's specific learning difficulties. Indeed at the time when I was doing this work the headmaster of the deaf school pleaded with me to put in my report that he was very much under-staffed, due to a shortage of specially trained teachers of the deaf.

The blind school admitted children as young as 3½ years, the deaf school and the school for children of mixed physical handicaps admitted between the ages of 5 and 7, the school for cerebral palsied children tended not to admit until children were around 9 or 10 years of age and very often they were 12 and 13 before they went to the school. This is largely because the school is intended for brighter children who will take public examinations and it has a specially qualified teaching staff for this purpose.

Most of the staff in all four schools felt that the school over-provided for the children. The comment 'we do everything for them here' was not uncommon and in one school this applied even to the provision of an entire wardrobe of both school uniform and informal clothes. The staff were of the opinion that this applied regardless of whether or not parents could afford to make this provision. It was often suggested that while aids to daily living were an advantage in a school where a tight time schedule had to be adhered to, it was pointed out that the outside world was not full of such aids, and perhaps the adaptation to life without them was made doubly difficult by having them within the school. This was brought out by the children, especially those in the two schools for physically handicapped where they thought that they were very much over-protected. A few staff thought that the schools over-protected their children, but they were unanimous in their belief that the parents were the villains of over-protection and went so far as to say that they had to indulge in a quiet, systematic process of educating the children to independence as far as their handicap permitted, and then convince the parents that their child was able to do a lot more for himself than the parents were willing to believe. Often a child's progress made during the school term was modified by the school holiday where the child had gone home and obviously had everything done for him. A number of the students agreed that their parents were over-protective and saw the school as a haven away from home. The number

of children who thought that other children played too great
a part in their life was surprising. Very few of the staff thought
this, but I am not sure what the children meant by this
remark. One thought I have on this subject is that for the
most part these children sleep in dormitories or at least in
rooms with other children and it could well be that they find
that this very much restricts their privacy.

Most of the children thought that they should be allowed
to make mistakes as any other child would and that they
would learn better and faster from doing so. While they all
urged this for themselves many suggested that others less able
than they might need advising. Staff also tended towards this
view, saying very often that no universal law could be applied
and that their action in guiding and advising children
depended to a very large extent on the individual involved.
The staff were inclined to tell the handicapped children that
they were much like any other child, but the majority of
children disbelieved anybody who said this to them.

An interesting moral dilemma was raised by many of the
staff who talked about the extent to which one should
protect the haemophiliac child. It would have been interesting
to have heard the views had there been a member of staff of
one of the schools who was himself a haemophiliac. Forty
per cent of the staff in the blind school were either blind
themselves or were partially sighted and these members of
staff took a consistently tougher line with the children
throughout the questionnaire. They were more inclined to
give a definite answer to questions by comparison to their
sighted counterparts. This showed up particularly when it
came to discussing future occupations for these children. The
blind staff were not afraid to tell a child that in their opinion
they would be unable to do a certain job upon leaving school
whereas the sighted staff would tend to shy away from a
definite 'no' answer.

Ever since special schools have been in existence, many
people have asked themselves whether or not the existence of

small communities with the common denominator of a similar handicap have not by their very nature created a barrier between themselves and the rest of the community, and sometimes this sense of isolation is increased by the geographical position of the school itself.

At first sight it would appear that the children and staff have opposing views on this subject, but on closer inspection I am not sure that this is the case. The children feel very strongly that they are isolated in a special boarding school and say that making friends with the community around is extremely difficult, and that only returning home for holidays means that they have to make extra efforts to keep up with their non-handicapped friends at home. Some also mentioned the time needed to re-establish contacts with parents and brothers and sisters.

There is also the question of the child being in a boarding school in the first place. In England, going to boarding school is largely a middle-class phenomenon and the concept of going away to school, with in some cases all the emotional and social stigma that this may imply to a family with a handicapped child, is entirely an alien one. In the normal course of events, most of these children would never have gone to a boarding school if they had not been handicapped and nor would any of their friends. This means that yet another form of common experience is missing between themselves, their brothers and sisters and their non-handicapped friends at home.

Staff do not for the most part consider isolation to be a big problem. Efforts to bring non-handicapped children into the school and for the school children to mix outside vary greatly from school to school, but staff generally agree that greater efforts should be made to integrate handicapped with non-handicapped children. They see the problems of the child's emotional immaturity as of great importance and feel that the majority of children in their care are extremely immature. One wonders to what extent this immaturity is a result of their isolation and difficulties in meeting other people. The problem of communication with other people is of particular concern to those children with speech defects who are all the while concerned and frustrated by their not being able to communicate and by being afraid that people will not be able to understand what they say.

The blind school has its particular pattern of dealing with the problem of social adaptation and a routine is almost set down on paper, since it is seen largely as one of confidence in mobility. The problem in the deaf schools is largely one of communication also, and in the physically handicapped schools the problem is very often both communication and mobility. Emotional immaturity and social adaptation are seen by the staff as being of paramount importance, more important even than the acquisition of academic skills. As one member of staff put it, 'the handicapped child has the greatest of all problems — if he is to get on in this life he must be socially acceptable, he must learn to smile, to laugh, to have as few mannerisms as possible so he does not stick out in a group like a "sore thumb".' I have been impressed with how well the students seem to accept their handicapping condition. This is because presumably staff generally under-stand the children's frustration in the acceptance of their handicap and see it as a problem with which they have to deal, and it is a problem which they seem to be able in most cases to go a long way towards solving.

The problem of the future for many of these children is an interesting one. The staff naturally enough are worried about their pupils' futures though they are right in thinking that generally the pupils themselves are not. It was suggested to me that once a family succeeded in having their child admitted to a special school, then that particular school, charity, or the state would look after the child for life. Maybe this attitude transmits itself to the children, though I have no evidence for assuming this.

I was rather surprised at the very high proportion of the

staff of all four schools who stated that they were practising Christians. For three of the schools, church on Sunday was compulsory — either a service was held in the school or children were expected to attend a local church. The children felt very strongly that going to church should not be compulsory, and for the most part they did not go to church when they went home for holidays. I would be interested to know whether there is such a high proportion of practising Christians among the staff at ordinary schools or whether it is a sense of vocation to help the so-called 'under-privileged' which takes the Christian into the field of special education. The religious views of the staff tended to reflect very much in their answering of questions about swearing, the telling of dirty stories and possibly their reaction to the questions concerning sex education and marriage of the handicapped.

Sex education at all four of these schools seems to be virtually non-existent judging by those members of staff I have spoken to, although they are all acutely aware of the many problems created for the handicapped by personal relationships, and would in most cases be ready and willing to deal with such problems. The children would ask anyone but a member of the school staff about matters concerning sex. This would seem to be a classic area where communication between staff and children has quite seriously broken down.

One school provided no sex education whatsoever and the newly arrived headmaster intended to do something about this quickly. The second school did have a marriage guidance counsellor visiting, but only a few members of staff realised this. In another school, I was solemnly told 'the headmaster takes the boys and the headmaster's wife the girls' for what sounded like birds and bees lecture, during the final week of the children's last term at school, and in the fourth there was a member of staff whose job it was to deal with sex education and related areas. Particularly interesting was the fact that old members of the school had been back and told him that he had to instruct the pupils on how to cope if somebody tried to 'pick them up'. He did this by getting the pupils to act out such a situation for themselves to see how they would react. It seems clear that nothing like sufficient attention was being paid to this all-important subject in at least three of these schools. We are just beginning to wake up to the problems of sex education for the handicapped. The Swedes have already been tackling this highly successfully for some time and it must be undertaken here too. Lack of good sex education only makes the handicapped person more emotionally immature and more vulnerable. Both he and his parents should receive advice, help and education on this all-important area of development as early as possible, as the following story illustrates.

During my visit to the school for the deaf I was talking to the headmaster when in walked the head girl of the school who was extremely attractive. She spoke with him and then left the room. He then turned to me and said: 'There you are, there is a problem for you, you tell me how I would solve it.' He proceeded to relate to me that this girl was very attached to one of the senior boys and he gave some detail of this attachment. He then told me that the deafness in both cases was due to a congenital defect. His dilemma was quite simple. From his knowledge of genetics, he thought it reasonable to assume that if this couple married the chances were very high of their producing a deaf child and his question to me was should he let this relationship go ahead or should he discourage it from the beginning for fear that this might very well be the end result.

This small incident shows up I think very well the dilemma with which staff in schools for the handicapped are faced, and one wonders to a very great extent to what degree these questions are really tackled by the staff, whether in the first place they are competent to do so, and also whether or not the children are willing to listen to the advice which is given to them. The blind school, of course, faced a different sort of problem in that in a boarding school where you have adolescent children, there is bound to be a certain amount of cuddling and kissing. I was amused to hear from one of the staff that in fact a time had been set aside on the school time-table for petting and one of the masters told me that this was known in the school as the 'geography lesson'. The staff in the blind school encountered a very real problem in this area since they had to try to convince the pupils, who were of course unable to see what was going on around them, that petting was normally not the sort of activity that was carried on in public!

In England recently there has been considerable disturbance in schools regarding rules and regulations, and particularly the wearing of school uniforms. In most cases children have been very much against it. I was somewhat surprised therefore to find in this survey that the staff were much more against school uniforms than the children, who really did not seem to mind it very much. The staff were of the opinion that it attracted attention to a handicapped child, but this of course would only apply to the vicinity in which the school is situated. The length of a boy's hair is still the subject of great dispute, as is the length of a girl's skirt.

The use of radio and television varies considerably from school to school; in the blind school both are very necessary as links with the outside world and in the deaf school some ingenious uses are made of television as a communication aid. In the cerebral palsy school television viewing is very much restricted by the headmaster and this is very much resented by the children.

I spent several days in each of the four schools involved, and from walking around the school and taking in its general atmosphere, and also from talking to various members of the staff, one is left with a very clear impression of the hierarchical structure and the general work pattern of each individual school.

It is quite clear to me both from this work and that done by other people in this area that the criteria by which the success of any learning institution are judged are highly dependent upon the way in whcih the staff see their own role, the way in which they see the roles of each other, and the way in which they see their relationship to the headmaster. This, of course, reflects in turn upon the headmaster's relationship between his management committee, or the local authority, or whoever happens to be in charge of his school, either from a general administrative or financial stand-point. The staff in all four schools were of the opinion that the people on their management committees were totally unaware of the problems which were encountered day by day in the school setting. In three of the schools the teachers and other members of the staff felt that they did not meet sufficiently often to discuss their common problems and would have liked very much to do so. Often care and treatment staff were not included in these meetings which were essentially the preserve of the teachers. I fail to see how a school can cope with the many and complex problems of the handicapped school child unless all staff involved with the child are included in such discussion groups. In the fourth school all categories of staff met together once a week and this was regarded as being extremely important, and indeed beneficial, by everybody. Without exception, the staff in the other three schools would very much welcome frequent multi-disciplinary staff meetings.

On the other side of the fence the children thought that the head boy together with the school's prefects ought to have more meetings with the rest of the pupils in order to discuss general school matters and other matters of interest.

Having listed some of the main points which have emerged, I would now like to make some general comments and then mention briefly an area of this work not so far mentioned which is of particular interest to me.

First, the staff in each school were generally surprised and pleased to find that staff in schools for other types of handicapped children experienced the same problems as they did.

In view of the deep concern expressed by both pupils and

staff in the problems of isolation and social adaptation (and indeed all staff were acutely aware of these difficulties), I wonder whether the problems of setting up boarding schools and/or day schools for both handicapped and non-handicapped children are insurmountable. If we were able to do this, it would go a long way to solving some of the many problems which seem to be created by the very nature of setting up communities solely for handicapped people. But how do we solve these problems?

There are broadly speaking two definitions of the term 'education'. The first is that of education for education's sake, the situation in which learning is a delight and an end in itself; the pursuit and acquisition of knowledge for its own sake. The second definition is generally regarded as being less respectable, but nevertheless tenable, that education is a means to an end, the end usually being whatever career the pupil has in mind, and in the case of many severely handi-capped people what type of residential placement they will need and indeed what will be available to them as adults.

We lay great stress upon social adaptation and independence as well as the common need for handicapped people to be able to communicate with and get on with the non-handi-capped. The staff know that determined efforts have to be made in these all-important areas, but often say that precious school work and routine prevents them from carrying out as much of this work as they would like. However, a very high proportion of handicapped children leave school and do not obtain employment, and I wonder very much therefore if the time has not come for us to take a long and careful look at the future of the curriculum for our handicapped children in schools. Should we not take a look at each child with all the experience at our command to postulate what his goal might reasonably be and then plan towards it? If the physical capabilities of a handicapped child are lower than his intellectual ones, but by pursuing a programme for his emotional and physical development and social integration to the full we find him a job, whereas the development of his intellectual capacity at the expense of the other areas does not find him a job, I wonder which goal the child would choose. Or should we ask ourselves a more radical question: would the integration of more heavily handicapped pupils in ordinary schools work, or would it pose more problems than it solves, and in that event, what is to be the future role of the special schools?

I am well aware of the difficulties involved in conducting a survey of this sort, but if it has done nothing else I think it has served to show two things. First, that the greatest problems experienced by this group of handicapped children are precisely those which relate to all the extra-mural activities which have to go on in order that these children can integrate into society, and it seems that the system as it is set up at the moment falls, in some places, very far short of this goal. Second, and to a very great extent this may be one of the main causes, there are quite considerable breakdowns in communication. A chasm exists between what the teachers think they are saying to the pupils and what the pupils are understanding the teachers to be saying.

I would like to end this paper by discussing briefly an area of this survey which illustrates this and which interests me in particular, and that is the area of, for want of better words, 'miss deeds' within the school and punishment for them.

In all four schools it was extremely difficult to get to the bottom of the school's rules and regulations. For the most part the staff said that there were very few rules and regulations in the four schools, with the exception of the blind school where there were strict regulations about mobility and for the purpose of this argument I shall disregard these. The dilemma is as follows. When I asked the staff in the four schools what sorts of misdemeanours were committed, they listed things like lying, rudeness, wasting time, bad language, cruelty to each other, bullying, disobedience, insolence, and two members of staff listed stealing. When I asked them what punishment would be meted out for these sorts of misdemeanours, I was told that punishment was not really necessary. On most occasions the children were given a talking-to and this was considered to be sufficient. Only two members of staff said that on occasions the children's privileges would be restricted. When I came to ask the children the same question, without exception the first item on their list of misdemeanours was stealing. Then they mentioned things like rudeness to staff, swearing, laziness, ringing the fire bell for a joke and being cheeky and things of this order. When it came to asking them what sorts of punishment they would be given, they were quite clear on this. The majority of them said that their privileges would be restricted and a few mentioned a telling-off from the headmaster. Some of them said they were gated, given lines and occasionally the cane was mentioned. In one school I was told of what was known generally as 'standing orders'. This was extra work to be done in the child's spare time. These standing orders were never mentioned to me by a single member of staff in the school in which this occurred.

There were many complaints from the children about restrictions concerning leaving the school grounds and times of going to bed and getting up. The boys in particular over the age of 18 thought it was grossly unfair that they should not be allowed to consume alcohol when by English law at 18 years one is legally entitled to do so. Smoking was a subject which also caused much controversy.

There are a number of possible explanations for these divergent views. First, the staff may not be willing to admit to an outsider, as I was to them, that they ever punished a handicapped child. They may see this as something which should not be done and if it is done should certainly never be admitted. Second, the staff may genuinely believe that they do not punish the children, and third they may just not remember that they do these sorts of things.

From the children's point of view, it is possible that they are imagining these punishments, though I rather doubt it. It is also possible that they had been told that if they commit certain misdeeds this is what would happen to them, and are therefore just repeating what members of staff have said to them and the third alternative is that they are in fact telling the truth! This illustration of one part of the survey seems to indicate clearly the sort of dilemma that schools, perhaps not only for the handicapped, are up against, and maybe this is a sure indication that those responsible for running schools and providing a curriculum for children growing up into adulthood would do well to consult very closely with their pupils.

8
An individual programme for behaviour modification

Lillemor Jernqvist

This paper is not a scientific work, but rather an illustrative example of how we try, at Bräcke Östergård, to organise the care of an individual at the school. Bräcke Östergård is a pre-school and ordinary common-school for motor-handicapped children. The paper will also show how we must integrate the different areas of treatment such as medical care and physio-therapy, as well as involving the staff at the hostel, for they act as 'stand-in' fathers and mothers during the week.

When we discuss the care of the individual we much too often talk about the ratio of special teachers to children in a particular class. Consequently we discuss the format of our work rather than the results of it. We hardly ever discuss the actual content. At the end of the year we report on the number of children who have been through our special classes and not the result of the treatment they receive. There are many reasons for this, the main one being tradition. Education as such is hard to evaluate and so we are not always sure of what our goal is, and, even if we are, we know that we may never reach it or that it is years away.

However, on the positive side, the experts are now discussing the content of special education more than ever before; and not only for the physically handicapped. It is absolutely necessary for all children. In this paper I shall discuss children who have behaviour problems.

In the Swedish curriculum the main area of concentration

has moved away from the quest for knowledge and facts, i.e. the stimulation of the intellect. We now also pay attention to the pupil 'as a whole' and combine reading and writing with emotional and social development. During the last few years, in two schools in Gothenburg, a symbol known as the 'School Rose' has been used. This has enabled us to evolve a more concrete and operational definition of the care of the individual within the curriculum. The 'School Rose' symbolises the identity of the individual. Each petal represents a cluster of variables which has to be considered whilst making plans for any particular pupil. The petals represent:

1 body function;
2 psychological function;
3 social situation;
4 citizenship;
5 working situation, and
6 leisure-time.

This may appear to complicate a simple idea, but it does help us in our work. We all need to speak about the same categories to ease communication. It also enables us to give the care of the individual not only content, but a more precise content. We achieve this through making observations and registrations that quantify the problem, thus enabling us to make small and exact goals.

After this analysis we have to give priority to some particular problems and also pick out one or two pupils to work with. We cannot handle more. Before making a final formulation of a problem we have to collect the relevant data. Let me give an example. A teacher has a great deal of trouble with a girl because she is always 'making noises' in the classroom. She shouts and speaks loudly; so much so that she is a severe disturbance to the other pupils. In order to make a concrete formulation of the problem we must systematically collect the relevant data. This may take three hours each day for five days. We then know that she is making an irrelevant noise, on average, forty-six times an hour. The final concrete formulation of the problem is therefore:

Girl makes irrelevant noise forty-six times per hour.
From this we can form the goal for the child's individual
programme. In this case it is quite simple: we want her to
be quieter; in most cases it is much more difficult.

We must take great care regarding which goal we set ourselves and ensure that it can be achieved through a natural
sequence of events. In doing this we must know what we
can dare to expect from the child and whether we will need
extra staff to achieve our goal. It is most important to make
the goal one which we want, rather than don't want! We have
to decide on the best way to achieve each goal, so that we
discuss each problem separately. Every person who works
with the child must be familiar with the final programme
so that we can all use the re-enforcement, thus handling the
child in the same way. It is possible that we may have to use
or construct different material (for example a new hearing-
aid) before a programme starts.

Carrying through the programme is, of course, the most
difficult part. It is very hard work to ensure that everyone,
from school to hostel, is systematic and consistent. Once we
have carried the programme through we have to evaluate
whether we reached our goal. What was good and what was
poor about the programme? We need to evaluate how the
personnel involved reacted. However, most important is to
evaluate the result, and in doing so, we must compare it
with the goal which we formulated and not with what is
considered 'normal'.

I will now relate one particular programme. It is grounded
on the learning theory models as they are presented by
Ullman and Krassner. They, in turn, use Skinner and his
theory of operant conditioning as their base. They use the
concepts of behaviour modification and precision teaching.
Operant learning is where the person has to respond before
he receives re-enforcement, whilst re-enforcement is a
positive consequence of behaviour — a piece of candy or a

smile. (For examples of the work of Ullman and Krassner see L.P. Ullman, 'Behaviour therapy as a social movement', and L. Krassner, 'Behaviour modification -- values and training', in C.M. Franks (ed.), *Behaviour Therapy: Appraisal and Status*, McGraw-Hill, 1969.)

Much of our behaviour repertoire is learned. For instance, if one analyses disturbances in the classroom one notices that all such behaviour is re-enforced with anger from the teacher. There are children who prefer attention derived from anger rather than no attention at all.

When a behaviour which is built up through re-enforcement diminishes and finally stops as a result of no re-enforcement, we call this an 'extinction process'. It is possible to replace one behaviour with a different one in this way. For example, children often receive attention when they are aggressive and this increases the possibility that they will be aggressive again. If they are consistently ignored when they become aggressive there is no re-enforcement process and there should be 'extinction'. Simultaneously, one can re-enforce the behaviour that one desires; for example, the more constructive behaviour of talking. Although attention and verbal praise are forms of re-enforcement, these are not always enough in social situations; sometimes candy, raisins, coins or tokens are needed to start the process.

Case example

T— is now 10 years old, but at the start of this method of training he was 8. He has spina bifida with hydrocephalus. He has diffuse brain damage and some so-called brain-injured behaviour is noticeable. He is not mentally retarded, but having spent his first years in hospital he was then moved to a special school for the mentally retarded. According to tests he is a little below normal IQ. He now spends his weekends and holidays with foster parents.

T— is a very active boy and cannot concentrate on his own. He is very aggressive and cannot play with other children. He knows very little about the world and has very poor language and so never starts a conversation. He lives in a small apartment in the hostel together with five other children who are more physically handicapped than he is.

Let me describe a typical day in T—'s life at the start of the treatment. He was woken up, washed and dressed and then had breakfast. All meals were sources of bad temper, fights and so on. He was unable to eat with the other children in the way in which the hostel staff would have liked. Although he could push his wheel-chair very well, he was pushed to school by one of the staff. School was a major cause of aggression; he hated it. After a great deal of fighting he finally arrived in the classroom where he began pushing over all the desks, throwing all the books on to the floor and quarrelling with the teacher. Occasionally there were things which interested him and then he was able to sit for a short period, but only if his teacher or her assistant was with him.

His day was full of conflicts. He wanted attention and tried to get it by shouting and telling people to go to hell. As a result nobody liked him, so he tried even harder.

I did a lot of systematic and unsystematic observations of his classroom situation and there were three outstanding aspects:

1. he showed goal-directed behaviour for thirty-five seconds at most, but the teacher had to help and watch him;
2. this goal-directed behaviour stopped the moment he was left, and
3. he always wanted to leave the school building and tried to escape.

At the hostel there were just as many problems. There were fights lasting thirty minutes whenever it was time to change his nappy. All meals were difficult because of his bad table-manners and because he was always interfering with the other children.

We decided to try to design an individual programme for
T—. After much discussion we all agreed on the following
approach. We would all use the principles of behaviour modification. We would not re-enforce the behaviour that was
undesirable, but would re-enforce the behaviour that we
wanted. This meant that we had to inform almost everyone
at Bräcke Östergård because T— moved about a lot and met
a lot of people. That was not an easy task as some people
believe that a naughty boy should be punished. However,
everyone did agree to handle T— in the following way: if he
was screaming, shouting or swearing he would be ignored;
when he was calm and nice he would receive attention and
love. He received re-enforcement whenever he was doing
something good, but none when he was fighting, although
one had to look after him so that he did not hurt himself or
others. If he became too dangerous we used 'time-out'; that
meant taking him away without comment and putting him in
a very dull place.

At the hostel we decided to treat two problems and hope
that they would transfer to school as well:
1   problems at meals, and
2   problems with changes of nappies.

1   The problems at meals we handled like this. We started
the programme in the kitchen. T— and one of the staff
would have lunch alone in the quiet of the kitchen, trying
to have an enjoyable time. T— would use the adult as a model.
He would then have lunch in the kitchen with one of the
children; then two children and then progress to eating with
the whole group. Here he would help himself to food so that
he could have as little as he wanted.
2   The fights over changing of nappies. T— agreed to a
system whereby he gained points each time he changed his
nappy without trouble; five points each time. He had a large
paper board on the wall where we marked the points on a
diagram. He could eventually change his points for the thing

he liked most — a trip in a car. Occasionally it is enough to
gain the points or tokens, but sometimes it must be possible
to change them into something. In such cases we must know
what the child really likes and in T—'s case this was trips in
a car. So that is what we chose and T— agreed to co-operate.
It worked; he gained more and more points and there was
less and less trouble. After ten weeks there were no problems
and the treatment stopped in a natural way.

At school to begin with he did not have lessons in the classroom. An assistant, an understanding young man who had
studied psychology at university, gave him individual lessons.
They sat alone in a very quiet room with no pictures, no
machines, no books. There were just plain walls, a chair and
a table. The room had no windows and that was very beneficial as T— was so interested in cars. They started by just being
together and playing with toys. They read books and news-
papers and talked to each other. After six weeks they started
with the pre-school programme, teaching T— the concepts
necessary for reading and number work. He became calmer
and a little more interested in learning; sometimes it was even
possible to have a short conversation with him. We had at last
established a little interest in school-work.

The next step was to get him into the classroom. That had
to be done bit by bit. We again used a system of points. He
gained points for passing through the corridor and getting to
the classroom door without trouble. Entry into the classroom
was the critical stage as the old stimuli returned. In order to
make this moment even more encouraging we made chalk-
marks on the floor; every stroke he passed without giving any
trouble gained him five points. He would then receive extra
points for sitting down at his desk.

The next goal was to get him to sit at his desk and work
without disturbing anyone. The teacher had a stop-watch
and gave him points for every three minutes that he managed
this. We used this treatment for thirty days and then I

undertook another period of observation. Leaving his desk happened many times during the first observation period and only eight times during the second. Making noises happened 135 times during the first period and thirty-six times during the second. A very striking change had taken place — T— now liked school and work. He now tried hard and was pleased when he succeeded.

We started work in January 1971 and during the months that followed we had many discussions in order to change the plans and to compare his old and new behaviour. Those discussions were very important because we became encouraged when we saw that the treatment was being successful. By 1972 T— was no longer a problem and we all relaxed. There were other children with problems and so we no longer paid so much attention to T—

Last autumn T— moved into a larger department with more children and new staff. They were not used to working in the manner which T— needed and his old pattern of behaviour returned. We have therefore had to start the discussions and planning again. The real difficulty is to find the time to follow every child with a programme year after year.

9

Integration of the maladjusted

John Wilson

In this brief paper I want to consider one or two general
points which, if I am right, apply across the board to the
integration into educational institutions of all minority
groups — physically and mentally handicapped, delinquent,
etc. I was first forced to think about this by having to integrate
a number of juvenile delinquents into a moderately traditional
British boarding school; but I shall refer to the particular
problems posed by this only en passant, for two reasons:
first, because I am under a vow of silence as regards almost all
the details of the operation, and second, because I imagine it
is the general conclusions applicable to any form of integration which will interest you, rather than the highly specialised
and somewhat peculiar version of the problem which I had to
face.

First, an important negative point. It is counter-productive,
and may be disastrous, merely to mix or integrate out of a
vague desire not to leave anybody out (a common guilt-
feeling amongst contemporary liberals), or a vague hope that
mere mixing will make everybody love each other (an infantile
fantasy found in hippie communes). An interview asked
British children at an international school based on these
lines whether their experience of French, German, Italian,
etc. children had not enlarged their tastes and tolerance. The
reply was 'Not a bit of it; now we know what the so-and-sos
are like, we'll take care to stay in England.' The first lesson

is: you can't do this just by making administrative or political moves, by 'going comprehensive' or just vaguely 'integrating'.

Administrative changes will work only if there is a change of attitude. This again cannot be effective by just talking about 'concern' or 'caring'; it requires a change of concepts. One aspect of such a change would be that our aim is to educate, rather than train or socialise. So long as we are concerned to turn out pupils who are good middle-class boys, or skilled technicians, or 'socially adjusted', or economically viable, or anything of that kind, then to that extent we necessarily stress differences of talent and performance. It is then that we find ourselves naturally slipping into the idea that various specialist services will plug the gaps: some people fail to come up to the norm of training and performance that we demand (because they are handicapped, old, stupid, delinquent or whatever), so we hive them off in special institutions and/or offer them the services of an ever-increasing band of specialist workers. (There are children being pursued by the probation officer, the school counsellor, the educational psychologist, the social workers of various kinds, the parish priest and the police, all at once — and they still slip through the net.) But if we keep to the notion of education, rather than adaptation to a particular social norm, we can resist this temptation. For, whereas we can train and adapt pupils for particular roles and performances, what we have to educate is people.

The value or worth of people, outside their social roles and performances, is basically the same; and this is why 'integration' makes sense. But the point has to be made explicit in the educational institution; and this means very considerable changes. It means, for instance, persuading upper middle-class boys to drop their concept of a person as someone who speaks with a particular accent and behaves in a particular way, and persuading working-class delinquents to drop their (very different) concept of a person, and educating them to concentrate on what is common to all people, on what defines a person, and to acquire the skills and abilities and attitudes relevant to this, and not so relevant to performance in examinations or on the rugger field.

Naturally this persuasion, this type of education, is not achieved by lecturing the pupils. It is achieved only by creating a particular social structure in the school, and building a good deal of the teaching and learning into such a structure. I do not see how it can be effectively done without a fairly small, potent group or 'house', calculated to attract the pupils' emotional investment more strongly than either the classroom or the street gang or any other social group. This requires certain arrangements which I have tried to spell out elsewhere (John Wilson, *Practical Methods of Moral Education*, Part 4, Heinemann, 1972); chief of these is the establishment of the system as more powerful than other features of the school (for example, the housemaster or houseparent more powerful than the academic staff). The administrative moves must be designed to this end.

From such a potent base the pupil can take advantage of whatever specialist services we can offer — and these will include the learning of subjects and other academic aspects of education, as well as the services of physiotherapists, psychotherapists, doctors, dentists and the man who keeps the boiler stoked. I want to stress that these people can only function effectively as specialists if there already exists a sort of extended-family or 'tribal' base of the kind I have (too briefly) described. Thus in the case of my particular experience, over half the problems which individuals had were dealt with by me (a non-specialist), simply on the basis of acting as a sort of father-figure: specialists were used, through me, only when really necessary and when the pupils really wanted their services. The whole relationships implied by talking of pupils 'being referred to' some specialist seemed to me grotesque.

I do not of course make any claims for my success in this particular operation, but it brought out the (surely obvious) fact that a large number of 'problems' required that the pupils be dealt with as people, rather than in particular roles (as law-breakers, exam. failures, handicapped, dyslexic, etc.). They needed attention and communication and understanding: given that, they might also need what we may call the techniques of various specialists, which could then easily be laid on. The fatal false move was to describe the person or pupil as 'a case of . . .'; not, obviously, that we cannot give such descriptions, but rather that these should not be the first descriptions, nor the first form of attention, that we give.

Even this, perhaps, conveys the wrong emphasis, for it suggests that we still picture pupils — particularly if handicapped or maladjusted in some way — as being permanently on the receiving end, being done things to, if not attended to by specialists then given 'concern' or 'care' by some benign father-figure. However, as soon as one takes seriously the idea of a family-type or tribal group, one can hardly avoid placing equal stress on another aspect: the duties (to use an unfashionable word) of the members as people, their social obligations, what they do and not just what is done to them. Most of the practical operation involves putting the responsibility on their shoulders, and very firmly too. Let them look after each other, as each may need looking after; let them do the work — perhaps even in very elementary ways, such as keeping the place clean, organising the food, the furniture and so on. Otherwise we have not a family or a tribe, but a depressing and spoiled bunch of dependent relatives.

It should be fairly clear how much revision of educational practice this entails. Thus, faced with tough delinquents whose idea of rules was primitive or non-existent on the one hand, and upper middle-class pupils with a largely unconscious idea of 'good form' or what was 'not done' on the other, there was no alternative but to get them, collectively, to work out for themselves what a reasonable set of community rules would look like — and contrast this with the (as I think) ridiculous idea of my trying to work this out with the help of various 'experts' in delinquency, sociologists, conferences on the 'integrated school', and so on, in an attempt to draw some blue-print of what we think would be suitable for them. All this involves a lot of blood, sweat and tears in practice — treating people as people rather than as recipients usually does — but it's the only way. The other way leads either to authoritarian regimes or to over-protective, guilt-laden ones; both of which, I think, are very evident in current practice.

I am not, of course, arguing that there should not be firm authority, firmly and, if necessary, fiercely exercised. To think that we can do without this is another liberal illusion, but it is not too difficult to work out, and ruthlessly enforce, the basic rules that a particular institution must have if it is to survive, and if it is to allow genuine education to go on. Having done this (and without too much argument being allowed to continue about it), we can turn our attention to the education itself; and this is where the practical interest lies. The questions are, I believe, mostly anthropological. What rituals and ceremonies bind the tribe (house, group, school) together? What work or play situations reinforce the importance of people as such, as against reinforcing social performance or roles? What concepts have the pupils to grasp, and what skills to develop? How do we change a person's self-image from some description like 'a Borstal boy' or 'a spastic' to something more like 'a person'? Very little research of any merit has been done here; some initial moves have been made, but much more is needed. (See Barry Sugarman, *The School and Moral Development*, Croom & Helm, 1973, and John Wilson, *The Assessment of Morality*, National Foundation for Educational Research, 1973.)

It would be possible, I suppose, to give some platitudinous account of what pupils learned in this sort of situation. They learn that 'no man is an island', that 'we are members one of another', that 'the working classes aren't so bad after all', that they can take their aggression out on the rugger field rather than on old ladies, that we all have our problems and our talents, and so on. I don't think there is much point in such descriptions. The difficulty is really this: it's much easier to be specific if we're thinking about social viability, roles, and performance. Trying to teach someone to walk, or talk, or pass 'O' Level English at once suggests certain practical measures, hiring certain specialists, and so on. Trying to teach people to see themselves and others as people leads us into the sort of platitudes and pious hopes I have tried to steer clear of. This is, au fond, because we are not ourselves as clear as we ought to be about a number of crucial concepts: the concept of a person, of a person's self-images and self-descriptions, of the 'practical syllogisms' (as Aristotle would say) which govern his thought and action, and of the concept of education itself (as against training, indoctrinating, curing, making socially viable, or just keeping quiet). I don't think there is any short way round the investigation of these concepts, and I don't think anyone who has not got a firm grip on them is likely to meet with much practical success — except by luck or intuition. So I would like to put in a plea for some hard philosophical or conceptual study here: it is the most 'practical' thing we can do, if we really want to be clear.

Equally it would be possible for me to regale you with some jolly anecdotes — 'I had one boy, a real tough he was when he started, but do you know, we got him to look after a guinea pig and he used to mend my wireless and after a few months he was as good as gold, it just shows how even the hardest cases . . .' — what one might call the Helen Keller approach. This is fun, and can be moving; but the real problem is to produce some working generalisations out of this fund of anecdotal experience — generalisations which are a bit more informative than saying 'It's all a matter of love.' As a point of methodology, I would recommend clearing the head, first (as I've already mentioned) by seeking a better grasp of the relevant concepts, and second, by imagining that one is on a desert island with a mixed bag of pupils — some spastics, some delinquents, some other minority groups, and some that we might jokingly describe as 'normal'. What would you do? What you would not do, I suspect, is hive them off to different bits of the island and start trying to 'adapt' them to some 'society' or other. Some prolonged thought about the alternatives might produce some striking results. Then, but only then, it will be time to re-enter what we call 'the real world', beset by public relations, inadequate space and staffing, pressing social needs which we can't just overlook, and so on. We have to think much more clearly about what we are trying to do. All I have tried to do is to offer a few generalisations, a few concepts, which need to be worked out in practice.

10
Emotional problems of the limb deficient child

Ian Fletcher

My remarks refer to the emotional problems of the limb deficient child but I am sure that much of what I have to say will be relevant to children with many other conditions.

Most of the problems are due to one fact and one fact only. When this fact is appreciated and understood by all who come into contact with the child, many of his troubles will either not occur or will be minimised and quickly overcome. I refer to the fact that the child is not considered to be normal. One might well ask what is normality! In medicine there is no such stage as normal, doctors recognise 'normal limits' and accept quite wide variations before pronouncing a condition of abnormality.

It is not sympathy or pity that handicapped people want but acceptance and understanding. They need full acceptance by their families, by their friends, by school-teachers and employers and, of course, by the general public with whom they are in constant contact. It will be noted that I use the word 'handicapped' rather than 'disabled'. People are not disabled until they are dead! Emphasis must be placed upon ability not dis-ability.

In my opinion the specialist who is to treat the child should see it with both parents as soon after the birth as possible. The future management can then be discussed in detail. It is extremely difficult for a young couple to accept a malformed baby into the family. It is, however, vitally important for the infant to have a good and stable home in which it can love and be loved. The child must be allowed to grow up as normally as possible and it must not be spoilt. He must be punished when naughty and there must be no unfairness, especially when there is another child in the family.

A child born with one or more limbs either missing or deformed has to make frequent visits to a prosthetic centre, particularly during the growing years. The first of its artificial limbs has to be fitted quite early in life, sometimes to aid the child, but occasionally to help the parents who do not like to see the infant with a limb missing. In my work there is a need for three types of treatment:

1 One must treat the patient's condition.
2 One must treat the patient as an individual.
3 One must treat the patient's relatives.

Number one is usually easy, it is number three which is difficult and takes so much time.

In the early weeks after the birth of the infant the mother is very conscious of the attitude of the general public, particularly if the limb malformation is obvious. It would help her a great deal if people would say, 'Oh, what a lovely baby', rather than, 'Oh, your baby has only one arm', a fact the mother knows only too well.

Small children may ask questions about the deformity and they should be given a rational explanation either by their own parents or by the affected child's parent. Children have to learn and they are likely to accept a reasonable explanation of the condition with understanding. If they are scolded or told to be quiet, a mystery is created and ultimately this will not benefit the handicapped child, who will be looked upon as an oddity instead of another ordinary human being.

Young school children usually accept a malformed child very well, but the 9-12-year-olds may occasionally make unkind remarks which can be very hurtful. When these comments are reported to the mother of the affected child she should make light of them, however much they hurt her. A child's security lies with its parents and when it is seen that they are unconcerned then many fears will disappear. School-teachers usually know if a handicapped child is suffering unduly and should then explain to the whole class that we are not all born alike. It is unwise to rebuke the children for making cruel comments — they should be 'schooled' not scolded.

Since the aim of all handicapped children is to be normal they should be encouraged to be normal. They should be allowed to take part in as many activities as possible and to wear fashionable clothes, even if some modification is necessary. Such alterations as are needed should be disguised as much as possible, particularly when the child approaches adolescence.

In Britain there are various youth organisations such as the Scout and Guide Associations. They accept handicapped children into their ranks and give great encouragement. Wherever possible the handicapped youngster joins in with the able-bodied although there are some special Packs or Troops only comprising of very severely handicapped boys or girls.

As mentioned earlier, the real problem is the fact that unless correctly handled at an early age the child grows up feeling different and often inferior to fellow beings. With good upbringing many have become outstanding citizens who have married and had 'normal' children.

How better to end this short paper than by quoting from Shakespeare's *Twelfth Night:*

> In Nature there's no blemish but the mind;
> None can be called deformed but the unkind.

11

Physically handicapped children in an ordinary primary school – a new dimension

K. W. Foster

First of all I think that I should qualify this title. I have never served in, nor visited, an 'ordinary primary school'. Whilst all schools serving the primary age range have similar curricula, similar pupil-teacher ratios, many common design features in the buildings, as well as common ground in the choice of books and apparatus and certainly the same age groups represented, the atmosphere of each individual primary school may well 'feel' quite different, even to one housed in a 'mirror-image' building, similarly equipped and situated only a mile away.

It is not surprising that there should be a special atmosphere within each school, because — almost unique to the English education system — there is so much freedom of choice left with the headteachers and the teaching staff. The staff will be made up of individuals who have been recruited into the service of that particular school, rather than drafted from a central pool. The children will be from homes within a single neighbourhood — and it is the social, economic and environmental forces of that particular neighbourhood which will influence the school's immediate aims, its social rules, its general atmosphere. By the very circumstances arising from the blending of so many adults and children within a distinct social region a school community will be born. It will grow and develop its own community character — how extensively, how purposefully, how confidentially, how happily, will depend so much on its leadership, its physical and social resources, and the support of the local education authority.

I, therefore, maintain that, whilst there is indeed a great deal of 'common ground' between primary schools, there can be no such animal as an 'ordinary school'. In fact, there have been such sweeping changes and 'new movements' in primary education within a single decade for there even to be extraordinary primary schools! I have started by emphasising the individualistic character of each primary school, because it is vitally important to consider a school's 'group personality' before any decision is made to establish a physically handi-capped unit within that school's organisation — or even to attempt to integrate a single handicapped child. A school may indeed be ideally placed geographically for physically handi-capped children to be more readily transported to and from school, it may be of a physical design and lay-out to enable physically handicapped children to move about with relative freedom, it may have a 'good neighbourhood' and therefore have few social stresses or problems with which to contend. Such factors may provide considerable initial advantage, and it might well be tempting to 'select' a school because of such apparent advantages.

If a choice was to be based solely on the logistic advantages (the form of the school building, the tone of the neighbour-hood and the material resources close at hand), there still remains the possibility, and therefore the risk, of failure.

What must be taken into account as an absolute priority is the individual and group attitudes of those people who will immediately be in the 'front line' from the moment physically handicapped children join a particular school. Headteachers genuinely do have a far more complex educational/social/administrative responsibility than once applied. Just as society at large has become more complex and generally more stress-ful, so has the micro-society of a primary school become more complex in its working programme, home-school involvements and out-of-school activities. Therefore, the headteacher must be a person who is genuinely in support of the inclusion — as full members of his or her school — of physically handicapped children. His has to be considered support, and it must be genuinely heartfelt support. That man or woman is the one person on whom the success of the intention will depend. It is that headteacher from day to day, from hour to hour, who will be accepting the direct responsibility for children with special needs, and also the responsibility for giving to his or her staff the support and confidence that is essential if physically handicapped children are to become true members of the school.

What then of the teaching staff? They have, by delegation, the responsibility, which can be considerable. They have to equate the 'double problem' of opening up physical and social opportunities for physically handicapped children to work and integrate with growing confidence within the intimacy of a primary classroom, and of ensuring that all the other children in their care do not 'lose out' as a result of 'rigging' the classroom programme to suit a tiny percentage of children with special needs.

You are, therefore, asking each teacher to share in additional responsibility and to work each and every day with the special needs always to be reckoned with. It is not a temporary role, but a conscious, permanent task. Above all you have to ensure that a teacher genuinely can face this commitment with belief and willingness. To organise it so that teachers must expect to have physically handicapped children in their care — part- or whole-time — is simply not good enough. Confidence has to be provided through personal guidance, prior consultation, and the opportunity to meet at first hand a physically handicapped child in a normal school programme.

It is, therefore, my contention that no organisation or profession — be it a local education authority, the various ranks of the medical profession, the voluntary bodies, etc.

— must even consider that they can set up any physically handicapped provision in any school unless the people who will bear the day-to-day responsibility in that school have genuine confidence and the spirit that says 'It is right that these children should share in our school's society — we will welcome them into membership'. No official body can require, impose or legislate for the establishment of physically handicapped provision within any school without the consent of the headteacher and his or her staff in confident agreement. To attempt to do so (however subtly) is to 'play with fire'.

How then can we ensure this principle that all human beings have a right — a definite right — to live in society to the limit of their powers and abilities? How can we develop the integration of physically handicapped children into the society of school with such confidence that they do indeed become a 'new dimension'? I will now try to put forward practical suggestions.

First, as trained, responsible adults we must establish real communication between ourselves so that we have joint practical appreciation of the common aims, and of the common problems to be shared. Let me provide one example of how two groups of people — each group concerned with its own particular service to children — can unintentionally create pressures. The medical experts can make a finely-balanced, competent assessment of an individual child's physical and/or mental ability to range beyond immediate medical care. Such professionals can also forecast, with a degree of confidence, a handicapped child's ability to handle certain physical tasks in conjunction with other normal children. The psychologist can assess a handicapped child's ability to cope with emotional stress, as well as its native ability to reason and reach a certain level of educational performance. Those trained as teachers are unlikely to be able to 'translate' the reports of the medical profession. They are unlikely to be able to gauge accurately the particular physical limits a child has reached prior to being considered for school entry. Nor can the individual teacher judge the amount of physical care (for example physiotherapy), and medical care (such as future treatment as a child grows or develops) without clear guidance.

Equally, the most highly qualified and experienced specialist, doctor or surgeon may have absolutely no comprehension of just what the role of a headteacher and of a class-teacher is in this day and age. There is the danger of advising or recommending that a physically handicapped child can safely attend school without any real awareness of just what that really means. The result can be that a child is placed at a disadvantage, even though the school staff are 'pulling out all the stops'.

These are early years as far as integration of handicapped people into society is concerned. It is surely a growing movement, but it depends, in the final analysis, on belief which is based on sound practical judgment. That judgment depends on the establishment of effective communication. I therefore urge this Conference to bear well in mind the need for communication between all agencies concerned with the placing of a child in a regular school situation — and add a plea that the medical profession might offer the translation of obscure terms as a gesture to teachers!

No headteacher should accept a directive to include a physically handicapped child into his school. In fact, no headteacher should be expected to accept such a child without the opportunity for studying all the background information and without consultation. This is because medical experts cannot give qualified advice on school placings without some attempt to gauge modern primary school life.

The members of the medical profession will probably continue to see the physically handicapped child at regular intervals, and this maintains continuity. The teacher with whom a child with special needs is placed (for part or the whole of each day) is committed for an extensive period of time, and will be in loco parentis. It is vital that the teacher can feel confident about full communication between all the special agencies dealing with that child.

My recommendations are that:

1 The school within which physically handicapped children will be placed must be selected with care — and through discussion with all concerned. The design of the building, its locality, and its type of neighbourhood are only some of the choice factors to be considered. The attitudes of the head-teacher and his staff, the atmosphere of the school, social relationships, etc. have all to be borne in mind.

2 There must be the physical resources to cater for these children's needs — special equipment to give mobility or to enable them to take part in educational programmes. Special accommodation which is part of the school is essential to the founding of a physically handicapped unit. To expect the teaching staff to undertake the care of children with special needs simply as an act of faith is just not good enough. It would overstrain staff not especially trained for the task, and impose strains on the other children who have an equal right to demand the teacher's time and energy. The costs of pro-viding adequate accommodation, necessary equipment and transport services in a day school is very much less than would be incurred in keeping handicapped children outside the daily life that they need to enter.

3 There must be adequate staffing — including welfare assistants. Without this the school is placed at risk.

4 There must be communication — clear effective communi-cation — between all concerned with the development and educational placing of physically handicapped children. This must apply before a child is placed in a school, and must continue throughout the primary school period. The main agencies are: the medical services, the local education author-ity, and social services (particularly when the child's family is in difficulty or over-stressed) and the headteacher of the school.

5 There must be co-operation borne of the realisation that

no single agency can meet all the needs of a physically handicapped child, and that each child will benefit from the shared
expertise of the profession — who will also offer their skills
on his behalf from birth to maturity.

Having expressed my views on the professional co-operation
that is so essential prior to placing physically handicapped
children in a normal primary school, and the vital need for
basic accommodation and special equipment to be counted
on by the school, I can turn — with personal enthusiasm —
to the experience which we have all shared within my own
school over the two-year period since the physically handicapped unit was first planned.

The 'new dimension' happened this way. The education
authority approved — in 1969 — a building programme that
would convert and extend the school premises to a design
that would help to develop a community school programme.
A design team was formed so that there would be a partner-
ship between the architects and those of us responsible for
establishing an extended school programme.

My own view was that a community school would need to
provide for:

1   the extension of home/school relationships;
2   student teachers and social workers;
3   children with special needs in company with the
     children of our council estate neighbourhood, and
4   hospitality to visitors and guests drawn from any of
     the education and social services. The aim was the
     creation of a school community composed of many
     people of varied ages, abilities, needs and interests.

It was planned that the group of physically handicapped
children should arrive to become members of the school on
the first day of the new school year — along with all the other
children starting their first day. (Temporary hutted accommodation was modified for the physically handicapped unit,
which they still occupy, but with the virtual certainty of
architect-planned accommodation by this autumn.)

The physically handicapped children arrived in their taxis, wondering where their fortunes had pitched them yet again. All the other children — new and old — arrived, and a tiny group of the physically handicapped children stared at hundreds of other children, and were stared back at. On that first day all of us passed a point of no return. The builders had gone, we had agreed to attempt the foundation of a community school, and we now had to learn to live together in a broader sense than just a formal school day.

It is easy to look back over this distance in time and remember what we had all been advised would be our initial problems:

1   The other children would feel sorry for them, or the sensitive ones would be upset by them, or they would upset the handicapped children by staring at them.

2   Parents in a neighbourhood like ours might resent 'having cripples mixed up with their own children' — even if there was only a total of 18.

3   Teachers in the main school would be in a risk situation if forced to deal with the immediate needs of a handicapped child and leave the whole class unsupervised.

4   The handicapped children themselves would lose confidence when they just had to watch passively as lots of other children of the same age did things that were quite beyond them. The contrast would be upsetting for any child with a major physical disability.

Although we did experience some snags and had to overcome a number of difficulties in the first few months, I can state — with absolute authority — that none of the problems of which we were warned have ever arisen. Looking back it is not difficult to appreciate why the transition was surprisingly smooth.

1   Juniors are, in general, very competent people. They are realists who can judge a person and assess a set of circumstances with surprising accuracy. It has never been necessary to explain 'handicapped children' in this school as the vast

majority of juniors had immediately worked it out for themselves. It must always be kept well in mind that only adults create social prejudices — colour, race, physical appearance, etc. It is only adults that educate growing children so that they inherit social prejudices. Children can be cruel as well as outstandingly generous in their thoughts, but their judgments are normally shrewd and without pretence.

So the children who came to us with obvious physical disabilities were very quickly accepted as children-who-are-different. Children who can crawl but not run, or children who can only control hand movements with difficulty, or children who are partially sighted or hard of hearing or without legs — but children. Being accepted by your peers is surely the most important form of acceptance, and these juniors soon became fellow juniors.

2   All of us were concerned with an attempt to create a school-home programme which needed the establishment of person-to-person communication, and we had no book of rules to tell us exactly how to do it. So all of us miscalculated from time to time, and all of us were learning to adjust to each other through trial and error. An entire school was involved in attempting new patterns of social relationship, and the physically handicapped children just formed a natural part of the whole.

3   The neighbourhood which this school serves was a helpful factor for, apparently, the wrong reasons. We have a considerable number of children with home problems of one kind or another, and these children are deprived in a number of ways. We have endeavoured, within the setting of the school, to give them security and purpose and, in general, most of this large number of children regard their school as a place in which they are accepted, and in which they can make their own individual contribution to a particular and clearly identified community. Quite apart from the teaching programme, a high percentage of the children are in school clubs, share in school organisations, go off on organised expeditions

and — as members of a community school — are the actual hosts who look after all our school guests.

It is because of their own social difficulties and their own social need for the school that the great majority of the children had a common relationship with physically handicapped children from the very beginning. These juniors — the oldest not quite eleven years old — could not only judge the physical needs of these newly arrived juniors confined to wheelchairs or calipers, but also quickly reasoned out for themselves that physically handicapped children are likely to have had very little real social experience. So here we had a natural situation in which many of the existing juniors could give support to physically handicapped children because they had also needed to find their own 'place in the sun'.

4   An increasing number of parents have begun to share in the normal life of the school — helping to run the library, assisting with reading groups, repairing books, acting as helpers on social occasions and going with teachers and classes on educational visits. This has resulted in first-hand knowledge of the way in which physically handicapped children get drawn into the general life of the school. So more and more parents — as well as children and teachers — do 'take these children for granted'.

These are reasons why the school is able to provide the social resources which will enable physically handicapped children to integrate to the limit of each individual's powers at any given time. It is an indication of what is possible if physically handicapped children are placed in an ordinary primary school, and this may be regarded as part of a 'new dimension'. However, it leaves the most important question of all to be answered — 'What contribution do physically handicapped children make to an ordinary primary school? ' From my own experience here, I feel my colleagues would accept the clear short answer — a great deal.

When you live with these children around you in the course of each school day, you come to realise how they make their own special contribution. Here are some reasons.

When you consider that all of these physically handicapped children have — throughout their infant years — known pain and stress and have seen concern, doubt and uncertainty in the eyes of the adults who they depend on for their intimate needs, whilst glimpsing only part of a normal child's world — you can immediately appreciate how adversity can develop particular characteristics.

Almost without exception these children of ours are Characters (spelt quite definitely with a capital 'C'). They have come to terms with themselves and, with each day, gain broader social experiences within the school at large. A number of them are specialists in playing practical jokes. C— has a bubbling sense of humour that ranges from the hilarious to the ridiculous, and she is never without company. S— is an expert on football teams, and has served as linesman at inter-school matches (pushed up and down in his wheelchair by his mate J— who is decidedly hard of hearing and partially sighted, very stubborn and extremely self-willed). P— and R— are the two stick-at-it characters who, once they have started on a project involving physical manipulation, will not give up. T— (who scoots around in a Chailey Chariot) is as sharp as a button when it comes to organising other juniors, and if she says 'jump' it is likely her followers will jump! And so on.

We have had some physical problems. For example, in fine weather at break times they go off with gangs of others and wander the whole of the school site — so that welfare assistants have to go out and chivvy them all back again. I have recently found it necessary to issue a proclamation to the effect that the Chariot Races being organised in the dinner times have to cease, as all the children involved are becoming a threat to the less extrovert juniors. The school grounds began to resemble scenes from *Ben Hur*! They share in assembly and social events, entertain a variety of visitors, have been shopping in the local supermarket, visited our neighbouring school, and mix freely within school group work during each week. (This sometimes leads to personal embarrassment because I have to explain to 'official visitors' — who expect them to be all together — that I am not really sure where they are in the school at any given time!)

I do become personally aware of them on occasions when I am feeling a bit fed up with things in general, for I wander into the physically handicapped rooms where they are perfectly willing to 'sort me out' and send me back to my proper tasks rejoicing. In conclusion, I can best sum up our shared experiences by saying that very few of us really remain aware of them as physically handicapped children. However, if — for some unaccountable reason — we gathered for assembly one day and found that they were no longer with us, the school would seem an odd and a poorer place. We need their contribution.

It is because we recognise a situation that has produced all-round social gain that we can look forward with confidence to the autumn months when it is fully expected architect-planned accommodation will make it possible to provide more places for these children. It is hoped that this community school will eventually include thirty-five to forty physically handicapped children within its membership. Two questions remain, and both questions can only be answered by society at large.

First, can any nation afford to waste any human potential? and second, how much practical thought and support are we giving to providing facilities so that the physically handicapped can best serve themselves and society?

12

Visually handicapped children in the infant school

Heather Jones

This paper is about a small number of young blind children who are beginning their education in the infant classes of their local primary schools. In some cases this means in their own village schools, and, in others, the local area schools for physically handicapped children. The children in the schools for physically handicapped in the main have spina bifida and became totally blind early in life following a blockage of the valve inserted to control hydrocephalus. I use the word blind rather than visually handicapped because in all cases the children have no effective residual vision useful in an educational situation.

There are several points I ought to make in order to emphasise the complexity of the situation with regard to the integration of visually handicapped children into the educational system for seeing children.

1   In October 1972 a significant report, *The Education of the Visually Handicapped* (HMSO), was published by the Committee of Enquiry appointed by the Secretary of State for Education and Science. In its consideration of the issues concerning education in ordinary schools the Report in paragraph 5.30 states,

The current trend is to emphasise that handicapped children are above all children, with many needs that children without handicaps have too. This approach however has its dangers as well as its merits, since it can lead to a demand that handicapped children should be given exactly the same educational treatment as other children; and we realise that it is impossible for visually-handicapped children to progress satisfactorily in a sighted school unless they are given special facilities.

2   Dr Michael Tobin, Director of the Research Centre for the Education of the Visually Handicapped, Birmingham University, has recently concluded an investigation into the attitudes of experienced teachers and trainee teachers towards the inclusion of visually handicapped children into normal classes (*The Teacher of the Blind*, College of Teachers of the Blind, 1972). All were non-specialist teachers, eighty in all, and they were asked to complete, anonymously, a rating scale consisting of questions relating to knowledge of, and preferences towards, eight groups of children with special needs. The groups were: educationally subnormal, the gifted, blind and partially sighted, deaf and hard of hearing, maladjusted, delinquent, physically handicapped, and the speech defective. The subjects were not informed that the main interest of the investigator was directed towards the visually handicapped.

In the table of results the blind and partially sighted were bottom of the list in terms of teaching preference and 'knowledge about'. This correlates with a relative unwillingness to accept the visually handicapped into an integrated group. Dr Tobin goes on to say that while it would be unwise to judge the question of integration solely on the basis of knowledge and attitudes current among teachers of the sighted, the success of the enterprise must depend to a very large extent on those teachers' competence and acceptance.

3   The education of the blind in this country has a long history — the first four schools were established before the end of the eighteenth century. They were all residential schools and this pattern was followed as more schools were built. As a result of this, virtually all the qualified teachers

of the blind are working in residential schools today and there are very few teachers available anywhere in the country who could assist in integrated education that is not associated with the residential schools. Allied to this point about the non-availability of specialist teachers is the fact that there are very few blind children in any one area. There were, in 1971, 1,207 children who were educationally blind and 2,335 partially sighted children receiving education at, or awaiting admission to, special schools for the visually handicapped.

4   Another point to bear in mind is the amount of preparation and production of equipment that has to be undertaken to make it possible for visually handicapped children to benefit properly from integrated education.

There have been two well organised and successful ventures whereby selected children continued to live at their residential schools while attending for secondary education at local schools. A few pupils from St Vincent's School for the Blind, Liverpool, have, since 1961, been going daily to take academic courses at local grammar schools, taking 'O' and 'A' Levels. Seven pupils from Tapton Mount School, Sheffield, have since 1969 attended a local comprehensive school, and some of them are taking 'O' Levels this year.

Quoting again from the 1972 report, 'The support services required to maintain a handful of children in the Comprehensive School are of a truly formidable extent and complexity.' At Sheffield, four groups (one of which consists of prisoners at Wakefield) and a large number of individuals transcribe into Braille a mass of material which includes foreign languages and mathematics along with the normal text books, etc. used in the school. Many people help with thermoform duplicating, others record texts on a cassette, one produces map outlines and College of Education students and others draw maps and text-book diagrams and make scientific and other apparatus. In order to keep up with the work of the comprehensive school the children themselves have to learn to work quickly, to type their homework, to study from tape-recorded material and to record their own notes. The pupils have a full-time resource teacher who, in addition to preparing work for each day, has to work during the evenings with the children.

The Liverpool scheme has needed just as much effort put into it — all the work has to be checked and unforeseen eventualities can occur — for example, a new teacher will occasionally change the text-books for the class, involving weeks of work transcribing them into Braille. There are qualified mobility teachers at both schools who have contributed significantly to the success of the schemes.

There are many other points to consider with regard to integrated education, but from the foregoing it will be clear that at present integration is for the few. For it to be of real benefit to the pupils there is a vast amount of on-going preparation of equipment to do, even when the facilities of a well organised and equipped school are available.

At Lickey Grange we have been concerned about small children whose homes are far away coming to a residential school at 5 years of age. Sometimes we have arranged for children just to come for one day each week, extending this, after a time, to an overnight stay and later to two days with one overnight, gradually increasing this to weekly boarding. Children whose homes are near enough, and for whom their local education authorities are prepared to provide transport, travel daily.

We like to get to know the families when the child is small and for this we have a pre-school service which provides information, help and guidance. Parents are encouraged to visit the school long before the children are ready to come and this means that they have some idea of the educational facilities provided. The most valuable part of this system is, of course, personal contacts that are made with the children at school and with the members of staff. The knowledge and assurance gained by these contacts make the change from home to school easier for everyone concerned. This service includes those children who begin their education in their local primary schools. At this moment in time we could not provide the resource teachers and all the other essentials for learning at the junior stage.

As part of the pre-school service, contacts are made with local playgroups and nursery schools so that, where a child can benefit from attending, any help necessary can be given to the group concerned. Joining in with the activities of seeing children and thereby gaining many of the experiences not often available at home is helpful. The children become used to being away from home for short periods and learn to accept new people happily. All this makes entry to school at 5 so much easier.

For some children, where everything is right — for the child, the parents and the rest of the family, where the headteacher of the local school is prepared to take the child for the first year or so, where the school governors and local education authority or school medical officer agree — we will supply advice, resource teaching and anything else necessary.

In almost every case the family is well known to the infant teacher before the child starts school — most of the children are in small village schools. The children in schools for the physically handicapped usually live some distance away but the teachers there are already used to children with a physical handicap and this is of considerable help in the beginning. Often the child has been in a playgroup with other children of his age and consequently knows most of the children starting primary school with him. Sometimes the child's mother has been the organiser or a helper at the pre-school group and knows the infant teacher well.

Before the child begins school at 5 we have already got to know the teacher of the younger group and have arranged a visit to Lickey Grange for her, supplied a certain amount of information and talked over the situation. She knows the help that we can supply and our ready availability. The two schools are kept in contact and visits, gifts and tapes exchanged. A lot of the equipment used in normal schools is the same as we use for teaching blind children — sometimes we may add to the provision.

Educational methods based on learning by experience are practised in all the schools we are associated with and these are ideal for blind children. Experienced teachers who normally do varied interesting work with their groups comment on how much the groups benefit from having a blind child as a member. It alerts them to making more use of the children's senses of smell, hearing and touch thereby adding depth to many learning situations. I would add that we have been particularly fortunate with the blind children's placement. We have a splendid group of interested teachers for whom the challenge of taking a blind child has proved both stimulating and satisfying.

Once the children are settled and beginning to progress in school we do not visit for a little while. This gives the teacher the opportunity to find out the child's ability. During this time she will be noting the problems and trying out various ideas we have given her. In this early period the child will have had training in touch discrimination and Braille letters will begin to appear on boxes, chairs, etc. The teacher and the other children know what these are as they have printed letters, too, so everyone is recognising them.

When the child is ready, we start teaching the beginnings of Braille and will have acquired the necessary machine for writing. (Soon the child will have its own illustrated book — with scratch scents and 'real' pictures.) The teacher will know a little Braille and in many cases so will the parents. We use different methods of teaching Braille for sighted adults. They learn to read Braille by sight as this is much quicker than learning by touch.

Braille is a slow and fairly complex system to learn. It is not just a symbol 'a' to print 'a' and 'b' for 'b'. It is a shorthand system based on a cell of six dots $\vdots\vdots$. Many signs can be made out of these dots, sometimes a group of dots stands for a word ending such as 'ment' or 'action'. The same symbol can mean different things according to its position in a word.

At present this project is still experimental. We have been organising it for a year or so and none of the children have yet come to Lickey Grange. We cannot assess its value in educational terms yet, but it seems likely that when the children come they will have a level of achievement at least equal to that of the children here and with the advantage of a longer period of home life and may, therefore, be more ready to benefit from a weekly boarding situation.

13

The social and educational problems of the young spina bifida child

K. M. Laurence
and E. R. Laurence

Medical aspects

Spina bifida is part of a family of conditions where the neural tube, which develops during the first four weeks after conception, has failed to close properly. This leads to local maldevelopment and degeneration of the neural tissue. Incomplete closure at the head end of this tube leads to anencephaly, the most serious of these abnormalities. These are always stillborn or die soon after birth. When the abnormality occurs a little lower down the neural tube, an encephalocele results. The encephalocele sac which takes its origin at the base or the head often contains brain tissue (the brain within the skull may also be abnormal), but sometimes such sacs contain fluid only. Especially if the sac is large it has to be removed because of the serious nursing problem it presents. A large proportion of such patients survive but tend to be extremely retarded, and although they do not usually have paralysis or incontinence, some are severely spastic. Defects of closure lower down the neural tube result in the common form of spina bifida cystica, which includes the myelocoele, sometimes known as the myelomeningocele, and the much less common meningocele. In the former the spinal cord is not properly formed at the point of the lesion and the cord tissue usually lies exposed on the surface. Such patients tend to suffer from varying degrees of leg paralysis and incontinence. The meningocele is a less serious condition, where no nerve elements are included in the sac. These patients are usually normal, or nearly so, and they have no paralysis or incontinence, and no hydrocephalus. The least serious of this family of conditions is spina bifida occulta which is very common, and is found radiologically in about 20 per cent of the population. It is usually of no clinical significance, though a few cases may have leg or urinary difficulties.

Multiple problems are often presented by a child born with the common and serious form, the myelocele. The head may be frankly hydrocephalic. Some hydrocephalus is present in nearly 68 per cent of these children even at birth, even though the head may not be obviously enlarged. This is due to an abnormality at the base of the brain, the Arnold-Chiari malformation, or it may be caused by other maldevelopments of the brain. The arms are usually normal at this stage, though as the child gets older inco-ordination or even paralysis, due in part to the malformation at the base of the brain, or due to the hydrocephalus, may develop. As well as paralysis of the legs and loss of sensation from the abnormal spinal cord with its myelocele, the legs and feet are frequently deformed. This is due to partial paralysis, where some muscles function while their antagonists do not, and this tends to pull the joints out of shape which results in such abnormalities as dislocation of the hip and club foot. Complete paralysis, on the other hand, does not cause deformity. The anus is usually patulous and urine may dribble because both anal and bladder sphincters are paralysed.

The surgeon will often close such a myelocele as a surgical emergency on the first day of life to help to prevent complications, because if nothing is done the myelocele soon becomes infected and becomes covered with pus. Additional damage to any functioning nerve tissue remaining in the myelocele may then occur resulting in even more severe paralysis, and ascending meningitis will usually set in which may cause death or brain damage, in addition to aggravating any hydrocephalus already present. The operation involves the removal of redundant membranous tissue, the fashioning of a covering for the spinal cord tissue from facial layers and the closure of the skin defect after undercutting judiciously. This is a relatively simple procedure and if all goes well the infant needs to be in hospital for only three weeks or so until the skin wound has healed. However, under certain circumstances some surgeons may feel that surgical intervention is not justifiable.

Hydrocephalus may be relatively mild, but often progresses rapidly until death, unless an operation is carried out. However, it may become arrested spontaneously but generally not without considerable thinning of the brain tissue with consequent brain damage. The relationship between the degree of hydrocephalus and intellectual performance is a fairly close one (see B.J. Tew and K.M. Laurence, 'The intelligence and attainments of spina bifida patients born in South Wales between 1956 and 1962. Studies in hydrocephalus and spina bifida', *Develop. Med. Child Neurol.*, 1972, supp. 27, 124-31). When hydrocephalus is not present the mean intelligence quotient is 100, but it is only 85 when there is moderate hydrocephalus, and as low as 71 if the hydrocephalus is severe. Various shunt operations are now performed to divert the fluid accumulating from the ventricles of the brain back into the blood stream and these prevent severe hydrocephalus. The most commonly used shunt operation in Europe is the 'Hotter' auriculo-ventriculostomy. Its insertion is a relatively simple procedure involving a hospital stay of less than two weeks, if all goes well. Unfortunately, this operation is not without its late complications, such as blockage, infection or just failure because of the growth of the child, and it often has to be revised several times over the years.

Urinary incontinence is not only socially undesirable, but may be severely damaging because back pressure may develop in the kidneys. If there is no back pressure in boys various penile collecting appliances may be used, but the situation is more difficult in girls, and one may have to be content with nappies and rubber pants. If there is back pressure, a urinary diversion operation may have to be resorted to in both sexes, with a urine-collection device strapped to the abdomen. If they are well managed this can be satisfactory.

Deformed feet and limb deformities are obviously not suitable for ambulation. Manipulations often soon after birth, repeated operations such as tendon transplants, muscle transplants, osteotomics and arthrodeses, some very extensive, may be required to get such children with varying degrees of paralysis ambulant. Braces, calipers and surgical boots may be needed to achieve ambulation. Intelligence and determination on the part of the child is a great help and so is the prevention of obesity. Many never achieve ambulation and may have to be content with a wheelchair existence. Ambulation is well nigh impossible if there is much mental retardation as well as paralysis.

Survival

In the past, few children with spina bifida cystica survived. In an investigation on 315 cases born in South Wales between 1956 and 1962 when little or no active treatment was given, less than eighteen per cent survivied to 8 years (see K.M. Laurence, C.O. Carter and P.A. David, 'The major central nervous system malformations in South Wales. Part I: Incidence, local variations and geographical factors', *British Journal of Preventive and Social Medicine*, 1968, 22, 146-60). Most died of meningitis or hydrocephalus, and a few died of renal failure. The few survivors were either very mildly affected, or were soon relegated to long-stay institutions, severely handicapped physically or retarded because of meningitis or hydrocephalus. As a result spina bifida was not

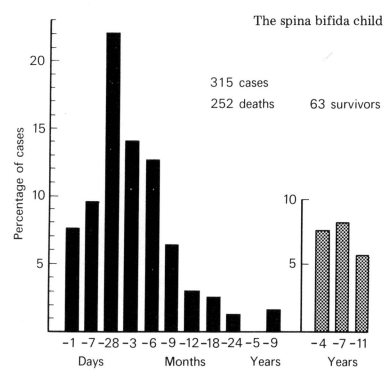

Figure 13.1 Histogram of the follow-up of 315 liveborn spina bifida infants born in South Wales between 1956 and 1962. Most of the infants died within one year, and only 18 per cent (15 per cent myeloceles) survived.

a very obtrusive problem, so few came into contact with it and even fewer came across cases in the school situation. Today, with active treatment of the spinal lesion, of the progressive hydrocephalus, of any meningitis and the prevention of renal failure, the situation is very different as a large proportion of the children survive. The medical and social services are now faced with pressing problems. The families are having to care for a child which may be severely handicapped, the schools are now having to accept this new disability, and the community will have to absorb many individuals with a new handicap. The incidence of spina bifida in Europe varies from less than 1.0 per 1,000 births in

Germany and France to 2.5 in England and Wales as a whole, and 4 per 1,000 in parts of South Wales. In England and Wales about 2,000 such infants are born each year, of which about 1,000 will survive to reach school age, five years later.

To investigate some of the problems generated by spina bifida within the family and also the community, a team consisting of Dr E.H. Hare, Professor K. Rawnsley (both psychiatrists), Dr K.M. Laurence, Mrs Helly Payne, a social worker, Mr Brian Tew, an educational psychologist, and Mrs E.R. Laurence, a research teacher, have been investigating longitudinally a cohort of 121 families, where a liveborn child with spina bifida, encephalocele or uncomplicated hydro-cephalus was born in South Wales between 1964 and 1966. For the families with a surviving index child at one year, control families were chosen, who were matched on the basis of the sex of the index child, position in the family, social class and area of residence. Mrs Payne visited the mothers soon after the birth, one month later, and thereafter at six-monthly intervals (see E.M. Hare, K.M. Laurence, H. Payne and K. Rawnsley, 'Spina bifida and family stress', *British Medical Journal*, 1966, 2, 757-60). When the child reached the age of 5 years, Mr Tew carried out a battery of intelligence and other tests, and Mrs Laurence subsequently visited the schools. The index children are now between 7 and 9 years of age, and the control children between 6 and 8 years of age. They are still under investigation, for this is an on-going study, which we hope to carry on until all these children have left school and are in employment.

Today all those with a meningocele are still alive, as one would expect. All are physically and mentally normal, or nearly so. One of the three hydrocephalics survives, and two of the six encephaloceles are alive, but all are severely mentally handicapped. Just under half of those with a myelocele have survived, mostly severely physically handicapped.

Most of those who died did so of meningitis or hydrocephalus. There were, however, eighteen deaths in children

Table 13.1   Survival of liveborn spina bifida children born 1964-6

	Died	Alive	Lost	Total
Encephalocele	4	2	—	6
Myelocele	54	47	2	103
Meningocele	—	9	—	9
Hydrocephalus	2	1	—	3
Total	60	59	2	121

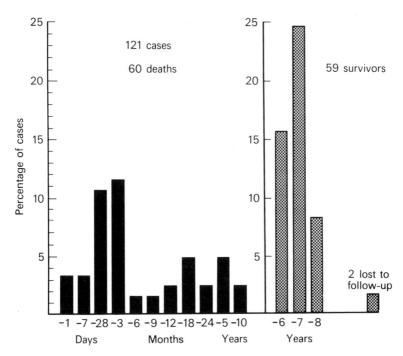

Figure 13.2   Histogram of the survival of 121 liveborn spina bifida children born between 1964 and 1966. Forty-nine per cent of these survived to 7 years (46 per cent of the myeloceles).

over one year, and these are of interest, as some of them have occurred at school age. Two died of meningitis, one died of untreated hydrocephalus, five, mostly the more severely retarded ones, died of bronchopneumonia, three died of renal failure and six died because of obstruction of the shunt which was inserted for the relief of hydrocephalus, and they usually died quite suddenly. One other child died during an operation to correct his squint. The survival of 49 per cent with modern active surgical approach compares favourably with 18 per cent when no active treatment was given. Fewer of these current cases have died in the early weeks of life (indeed this was the chief aim of the therapeutic efforts), but more died of late complications. It is likely that some more will die during the next few years due to the sort of causes enumerated above.

Social problems

The family is faced with various problems. The shock of having an abnormal baby is the first in the chain. To overcome this the parents need much sympathy, help and understanding. This is followed immediately by the need for surgery, generally at a centre some distance from the maternity unit, with the consequent separation of mother and child. After this admission, which is usually not far less than three weeks, there follow repeated hospital attendances and in-patient admissions for surveillance and treatment for the next few years. The families are generally perplexed by what is happening and what is to become of their child. They frequently get different and conflicting explanations and advice from the many specialists, the neurosurgeon, the paediatrician, the orthopaedic surgeon, the urologists, the physiotherapists, the social workers, to mention just a few, which add to their problems. However, there is often not enough time available for hospital staff to explain adequately and fully. More time should be found. They have to contend with the questions and remarks of relatives, friends and neighbours, who however, in our community, tend to be supportive. They have worries about the future. In view of the many medical and surgical problems the parents will naturally have worries about the child's survival, but more important about the quality of his life and later about his education. They will more than likely have to face financial worries for transportation of their handicapped child, for aids and appliances and house modification to enable them to cope with him, and so on. Most parents will also have fears of a possible recurrence of a similar malformation in a future pregnancy. All these stresses, which generally worsen rather than improve, will inevitably create disharmony in some families and occasionally lead to marriage break-up.

The social problems of the child himself at school-entry age and after fall into six broad categories which are physical isolation, repeated hospital attendances and hospitalisation, family tensions, incontinence, possibly having to go to a special or even a residential school, and having to measure up to the unrealistically high expectations of his parents.

The more fortunate children are ambulant with relatively little treatment or just with short leg irons or surgical boots, while others have to wear cumbersome full-length braces and use crutches. However, many have to be content with a wheelchair existence. They are unable to get about like normal children and so cannot join in play and gain the experience that a normal child obtains from exploration and the rough and tumble of a normal association with other children. As the child gets older parents may find it increasingly difficult to take him out on shopping expeditions, especially if this involves pushing a heavy child in a wheelchair up hills, or up and down many steps, or on and off public transport. As a result many children with spina bifida are not fully socialised by the time they are expected to go to school at the age of 5 years. Increased facilities for nursery schooling from as early as 2 years would help to alleviate this problem. Rehousing of some parents who are in difficult, perhaps hilly, areas would be a considerable help, and a bungalow is preferable to a house.

Parents with a severely handicapped spina bifida child are generally worried about the child's health and his future. An untoward amount of parental attention is often expended upon the child, which may lead him to become self-centred and spoilt. The other children in the family may become neglected and show emotional disturbance, as has been the finding in our study. Parents are often involved in the extra expense entailed in modifying their home to enable a handicapped child to get from room to room, and perhaps in installing a downstairs bathroom and toilet to make the care of the child less arduous. Some parents have felt the need to obtain a family car, although well beyond their means, in order to enable the handicapped child to be transported. Often considerable loss of work and additional expense is incurred when their handicapped child has to attend hospital out-patient clinics, or be admitted to hospital for treatment and one or both parents has to be with the child.

Family stress after the initial shock seems to become acute again about the time when a normal child should be ambulant and clean and dry, and again at about 4 years old, the time when they become acutely concerned about education. Further times of acute stress will probably occur when the change from junior school to secondary school takes place, and doubtless during adolescence and when school-leaving time approaches and an 'occupation' will have to be found. Although the family units tended to be more united after the birth of the handicapped child than the control families, as the problems mounted and the tensions increased the number of broken marriages or unions under severe tension amongst the index families increased rapidly, and overtook those found in the control families when the children reached school age. Such family stresses inevitably are paralleled by tensions and stresses in the child himself.

Most parents and many children become acutely anxious about out-patient hospital attendances, and of course more so about in-patient admissions. Not only do hospital admissions represent a break with familiar family or school surroundings, but they also represent an interruption in normal routines and education. Many children return from hospital disturbed and having lost considerable ground, which is sometimes not easily made up.

Many of these children are incontinent. When this is associated with back pressure of urine, renal damage through back pressure alone, or through repeated urinary infection there is a constant danger. Under these circumstances a urinary-diversion operation with the formation of an artificial bladder has to be undertaken. Urinary-diversion operations had been thought to be the answer to the social problem of incontinence, as a well managed diversion operation can leave the patient perfectly acceptable socially. However, these operations have proved to be far less satisfactory in the long term than had been anticipated, and now fewer are carried out for purely social reasons. Faecal incontinence as opposed to urinary incontinence is less of a problem and can usually be managed adequately by straightforward medical methods. What effect incontinence and its sexual sequelae have upon the child psyche has not yet been assessed, but the consequences must be profound.

The educational needs of the child are sometimes such that special schooling is required, as will be shown. In isolated areas this may well mean a residential school with the necessity of separation from the family for the whole week, with only weekends at home, or sometimes even for the whole term, with only the holidays at home. Separation from the family may also be forced by that family's need to take a holiday away from the handicapped child, either because the family requires the 'rest' or because of the family's inability to find anywhere suitable to go with the handicapped child.

Finally, parents and occasionally teachers, as will be shown, sometimes have unrealistically high expectations of the children, either because they do not appreciate the child's handicap, or they are unable to come to terms with it. Under these circumstances the child will always labour under difficulties and may possibly feel a failure.

Educational problems

It used to be assumed that spina bifida patients had a normal distribution of intelligence and that they had normal upper limb function (see P. Henderson, 'The educational problems of myelomeningocele', *Hospital Medicine*, 1968, 2, 909-14). In the comparison of the Full Scale IQ on the Weschler Pre-School Scale for fifty-nine spina bifida children born in South Wales between 1964 and 1966, the survivors of the 121 live-born cases and fifty-six controls, it has been shown that there is a significant difference in the distribution of results.

The results of the normal group are almost symmetrical with about the same number of children one standard deviation above and below the mean. Two cases fall below this distribution range and thus illustrate some of the difficulties which can arise when controls are matched at birth. One case is a boy with an IQ of 76 who was diagnosed as having cerebral palsy when he was 18 months old. The second is a girl who had a normal development up to the age of 2 but then developed cerebral meningitis, which produced hydrocephalus and much brain damage. She has a Full Scale IQ of 40. In spite of these two typical scores the mean Full Scale IQ of the control group is about 104. These results are in close agreement with other British normative studies. The scores of the spina bifida population are skewed towards the lower end of the IQ range, with a peak of scores in the dull and backward range of intelligence. Twenty children had IQ scores below 70 and twenty-four above 85, eight of these

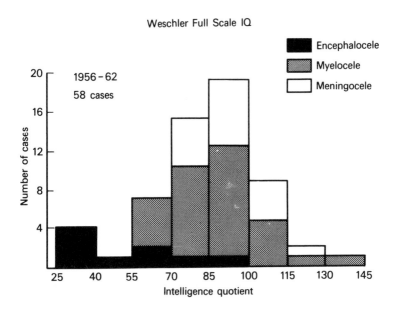

Figure 13.3   Histogram of the IQ results of fifty-eight spina bifida and fifty-six control children. The means of 78 and 104 respectively are indicated.

being meningoceles who will be considered separately presently. Taking the population as a whole the Full Scale IQ is almost 78. The twenty-six-point IQ difference between index and control groups is statistically significant. Spina bifida children thus often have a considerable intellectual deficit.

It is important to look at the diagnostic groups separately, as the various types of lesion are associated with specific sequelae, both physical and psychological. The nine meningocele patients show little difference from the control population, with the Weschler Full Scale mean IQ of 101. Neither mentally nor physically are they likely to be distinguishable from a normal school population. The myeloceles represent the largest category of cases. Their peak of scores is similar to

121

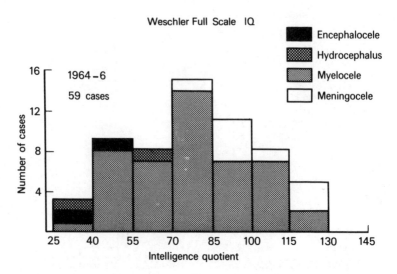

Figure 13.4   Distribution of IQ scores of fifty-nine spina bifida children divided up according to type of lesion.

that of the whole spina bifida population. Sixteen cases, or one-third of the group, have IQs below 70, while at the other end of the scale there are nine cases (or 20 per cent of the group) who have IQs in excess of 100, their mean Weschler IQ score being 77. The two cases of encephalocele and the one case of hydrocephalus were all very severely retarded.

    To give further support to the view that children with spina bifida are abnormally distributed in intelligence one might quote our study of relatively untreated patients born between 1956 and 1962 (see Tew and Laurence, op.cit., and K.M. Laurence and B.J. Tew, 'The natural history of spina bifida cystica and cranium bifidum cysticum; the central nervous system malformations in South Wales, part 4', *Archives of Diseases in Childhood*, 1971, 46, 328-38). This group was first seen in 1966 and then re-examined in 1972. In the six years between testings, two-thirds of the cases remained within ten IQ points of their original score. The results of the three clinical groups are similar to those found

122

in our current study. The nine encephaloceles are, on the whole, very severely retarded with a mean Full Scale of 52. The mean IQ of the myeloceles is 84, while the mean IQ of the meningoceles is 94. Again the distribution overall skewed towards the lower end of the scale, indicating that the spina bifida group show evidence of intellectual damage. It was also shown that in 1966 the IQ scores of the females were significantly lower than those of the males. When re-examined in 1972 it was found that the scores between the sexes had widened further. The results of our current study show the same trend, although there is a small difference between the sexes due to a slightly lower mean IQ in males, and in fact the sex difference resembles a normal population more closely than that of a handicapped group.

Table 13.2   Sex difference in IQ scores (WPPSI Full Scale)

	Males	Females
1956-62 cohort	93	73
1964-6 cohort	83	74
1964-6 controls	108	104

Finding that girls are intellectually poorer than boys is unusual and as far as we know spina bifida is the only handicapping condition in childhood where girls have a poorer intellectual outlook. Many other studies, for example, cerebral palsy, mental retardation, speech defect, reading retardation, maladjustment, to name but a few, found that boys are more damaged or vulnerable than girls (see M. Rutter, J. Tizard and K. Whitmore, *Education, Health and Behaviour*, Longmans, 1970, and R. Davie, N. Butler and H. Goldstein, *From Birth to Seven*, National Children's Bureau, 1972). Spina bifida is known not only to be more frequent in females (P.A. Doran

123

and A.N. Guthkelch, 'Studies in spina bifida cystica. General survey and reassessment of the problem', *J. Neurol. Neurosurg. Psychiat.*, 1972, 24, 331-45) but also appears to have more damaging consequences both physically and also intellectually. The reasons for this remain obscure.

The second assumption that has to be questioned is the view that spina bifida cases have normal upper limbs. It has been shown that the Arnold-Chiari malformation which is so frequently present in spina bifida can produce upper-limb dysfunction in the form of paralysis and inco-ordination. In addition, any teacher who has had young spina bifida children in her care must have observed that there is frequent lateral confusion, loss of fine finger control, and lack of visiospatial perception.

The whole population of late-treated cases from our 1956-62 series were given tests of reading, spelling and arithmetic; an attainment age of 11 months above or below chronological age was accepted as being within normal limits and the range of scores was confined to four years discrepancy or less between the reading, spelling and arithmetic ages, to two years achievement in advance of chronological age. It is clear that there is a high inter-correlation of achievement and failure in these three skills. The skewed distribution of the lower end of the scale is accounted for in part by the nil scores of most of the encephaloceles. The females again contribute more to retardation in attainment than males. Three times more boys than girls read at their age level or above and twice as many boys function at their age group level or above in arithmetic. In spelling there is less of a difference with boys showing their superiority by one half.

Parents often come to terms with their child's physical handicap in a realistic manner over a period of time, but the evidence of mental handicap in addition to physical disability is not similarly acknowledged. Indeed when this was examined at the time of the re-testing of our 1956-62 sample in older children, we asked the parents to estimate their child's

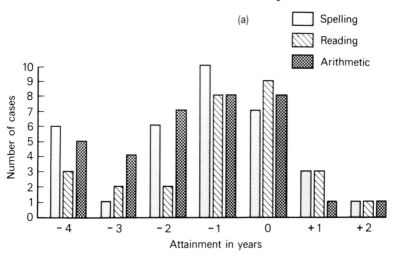

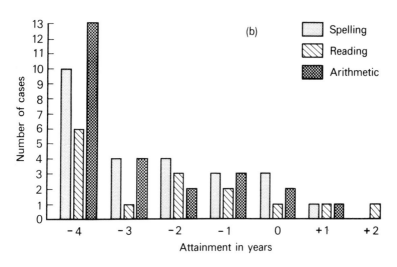

Figure 13.5(a) and (b)   Histogram of the attainment of fifty-eight children born between 1956 and 1962, divided up according to whether their performance is above or below the normal expectation for the age; (a) thirty-four boys, (b) twenty-four girls.

125

mental age in years and months. This estimate was converted into an IQ score and then compared with the Weschler Scale IQ. In hardly any cases did the parents under-value their child. The results indicate that when the child was at the extreme end of the IQ range the parents were able to make a more realistic assessment. However, 39 per cent of the parents were more than sixteen IQ points away from the Weschler scores, with some parents estimating their child to be up to forty IQ points higher. The greatest degree of distortion occurred when the child was in the 50-80 IQ range with the parents judging their child as in the normal or near-normal range of intelligence. This was particularly so when the child showed evidence of the so-called 'Cocktail party syndrome' (see B. Hagberg and L. Sjogren, 'The chronic brain syndrome of infantile hydrocephalus', *Amer. J. Dis. Child*, 1966, 112, 189-96). This is a learning disability almost specific to hydrocephalic children and consists of a particularly mature type of speech which appears on first hearing to be meaningful but with increasing familiarity is found to be no more than mere verbosity. The child's hyper-verbal behaviour is frequently accompanied by a selectively good memory, usually for social events. Very often the parents think that their child is more than compensating for his immobility by achieving in other directions. Such children are difficult to teach as their chatter frequently disturbs other pupils in the class. In addition they rely on their charm to divert the teacher from the task of encouraging learning towards less threatening social activities. As this syndrome is commonly associated with brain damage, difficulties in maintaining attention and concentration also combine to affect the learning process. The unrealistic expectation which many of the parents have can only add to the difficulties and frustrations and educational problems of the children.

As the spina bifida child often has extensive surgical treatment until he is of late junior school age, school attendance can be irregular. If we consider in addition the combined effects of hydrocephalus, cerebral damage, visual abnormalities, limited social experience, poor motivation and an IQ lower than average, this group of patients are educationally at risk. In a recent report (*The Health of the School Child 1966-68*, HMSO, 1969) it was estimated that in South Wales 50 per cent of spina bifida cases who survived infancy may require special educational provision. Our data derived from the relatively untreated cases born between 1956 and 1962 and our current investigation suggests a higher figure. We estimate that between two-thirds and three-quarters of the survivors will eventually require special educational assistance.

School placement

Study into the social and psychological problems of the family with the spina bifida child has now been extended into the school situation of the fifty-nine survivors in an attempt to estimate the success of placement of handicapped children in various types of schools and to understand the attitudes of teachers and children and the problems involved. It has enabled us to look at children both in special schools and in primary schools, and to measure the success of placement. Of the fifty-nine surviving children, fifty-six have been visited in their schools.

Table 13.3   Present school placement of fifty-six spina bifida children

		Primary school	Special school
Meningocele	9	9	—
Myelocele	44	17	27
Encephalocele	2	—	2
Hydrocephalus	1	1	—
Total	56	27	29

As one would expect, the meningoceles, or those without nerve tissue involvement, are all placed in primary schools. Of the children with a myelocele, most of whom have some nerve tissue involvement and therefore some degree of paralysis or incontinence, or both, and often some hydrocephalus, seventeen are in primary schools and twenty-seven in special schools. The IQ range of the former is from 62 to 124 with a mean of 91, that of the latter ranges from 44 to 106 with a mean of 69. Two encephaloceles, both severely retarded, are in special day schools, and one child with hydrocephalus unassociated with spina bifida attends a primary school.

In the beginning, the problem was one of winning acceptance for their children, and buoyed with the feeling at the time that their children, though physically handicapped, fell within the intelligence scatter of the normal population, early attempts were made to place children in the local schools. Many bitter and sad stories are still told of parents and bewildered teachers facing an altogether new problem for which they were not yet equipped either by training or by support from medical or educational authorities or the social services.

Application for admission to primary schools was made by the Medical Officer of Health, the psychologist or by parents, who sometimes put pressure on the headmistress, and often presented her for the first time with a severely handicapped child. Hesitation, while the headmistress is assessing the needs of the child or the facilities she can offer, has been read as refusal to accept the child. Add to this the old authoritarian image some parents still have of the teacher, together with their often unrealistic expectations for their child, and you have a situation which colours the difficult beginning of a school life.

Here one might note the changed role of the nurse, who in the past acted as a valuable link between home and school. She had often visited the family and in difficult cases acted as a welfare officer bringing school and parents together in

the interest of the child. Now that nurses are no longer
attached to a district but to general practices this continuity
and personal touch is lacking, her visits to schools being less
frequent. A succession of nurses may well take the place of
one.

Teachers in the schools of the control children when faced
with the hypothetical problem of a handicapped child tended
to worry most about problems of toileting and large classes.
The following figures about the teachers of the spina bifida
children support their fears. Twenty-two spina bifida children
were placed in classes of up to seventeen pupils and all these
classes had from one to four nursery assistants. These were
all in special schools. There were twelve children placed in
classes of twenty-one to twenty-nine and none of these had a
nursery assistant, but in two instances there was some extra
teaching help. Twenty-one children were placed in classes of
thirty to forty and only one of these had full-time nursery
assistance, though three more had nursery assistants, but these
were shared between five and six classes. In addition, one
child who came to school with little speech and unable to
walk has an extra part-time teacher to himself.

Whenever possible in infants' schools, it seems that the
toileting problem is dealt with by the child going home at
lunchtime. Very often if he has a urinary diversion, all has to
be well until mother can take care of it, or a telephone call
summons the mother to school, either to deal promptly with
the problem or to remove the child. Where a child does stay
to lunch the willing 'dinner ladies' help, or he is even taken
home by one of them and cared for, since there are no
facilities in the school, and home is too far away.

Difficulties in school buildings must be considered, especially level floors and accessibility of toilets and water, hot
if possible. The problem presented by steps may be overcome
with the help of a carpenter. The playground is important,
for a school with a sloping playground prevents a chairbound
child from going outside to play with the others. Experience

outside the classroom may be denied to some of the chair-bound children in primary schools through fear, or lack of enough adult supervision.

Regarding the ability of the children, teachers were asked what skills the child had when he first came to school, whether he could use a pencil, recognise his name, recognise numbers or put on his coat. Half of the children were not able to perform any or only one of these four skills. Teachers were also asked to assess the child's work, and this correlated favourably with the psychologist's reports. Five were assessed above average, thirteen as average, and thirty-three below average.

Once the child started day school, settling in seems to have presented few problems, but those fortunate enough to have attended a nursery for the handicapped made the transition very smoothly indeed. There are no complaints about sociability. Spina bifida children are too ready to communicate, even though their communication is sometimes without much content. Only two children showed some difficulty and one became withdrawn after a long stay in hospital.

The advantages of special schools over primary schools for some of the severely physically handicapped are becoming obvious, especially when this is associated with some degree of mental backwardness. First of all there are specially trained or experienced teachers. Classes are small, some have fifteen pupils, some as few as nine. There is co-operation with medical staff and services, which in primary schools is lacking. Once a child is placed in a primary school there is often little further support or evident interest forthcoming and little or no information either by way of assessment on medical reports. Children often have to be taken out of primary school for visits to clinics or for regular physiotherapy, or do without. On the other hand, this is made available in the schools for the physically handicapped. However, the four walls of the classroom do confine the special school child to a little world, however exciting and stimulating, while his companions enjoy the freedom of the playground and the open air, growing daily more self-confident.

The children who have tried to start in a primary school and have gradually found their way into special education underline the importance and place of special schools. The thirty-three spina bifida children who were originally placed in primary schools had an IQ range from 50 to 124, the mean being 91.1. The twenty-three children in special schools ranged from 35 to 106 with a mean IQ of 67.3. Only incontinence of urine, in the opinion of his teacher, was keeping one boy with an IQ of 106 in a special school. Six children in all have been transferred to special schools with IQs ranging from 44 to 77, the mean being 63. This made little difference to the mean IQ of children in special schools, but the mean IQ in primary schools becomes 97 instead of 91.

One child not physically handicapped was transferred because of her mental retardation, IQ 72. The remaining five children were both physically and mentally severely disabled. There was growing realisation by the infants' staff that these children needed more than they were able to give. Among other problems the tendency to overweight in spina bifida children made them increasingly difficult to lift in and out of their chairs. Two of the mothers were rejecting their children, and this was the precipitating factor in their emergency transfer, along with poor social background.

No mention has been made here of special units attached to primary schools, since only one, an assessment class, and so a temporary measure, came within our study, but this could well go part of the way to keeping our handicapped people within the community, to the satisfaction of parents unwilling to send their children to a residential school.

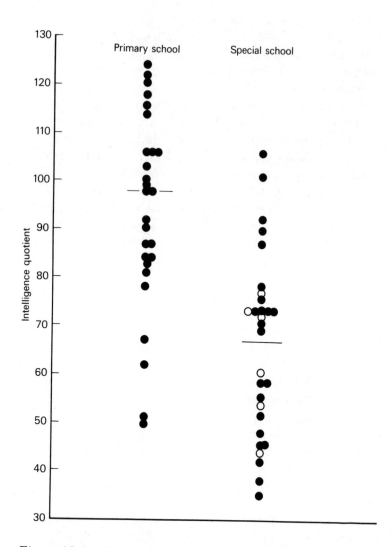

Figure 13.6 Scattergram of IQ results of fifty-six spina bifida children, separated into two columns according to their present school placement. The six children who started in a primary school but had to be transferred are indicated by open circles.

Summary

It is quite clear that help for the families is required in the form of sympathetic advice and information in hospital. Real social work support at home and financial help is also needed. Possible house modification or rehousing would do much to provide a better environment for the affected children in some cases. Nursery schooling would do much to help with socialisation of children who become isolated all too easily. The educational needs and problems must be appreciated and taken into account and the children should then be given the kind of schooling most appropriate. This may be in the normal local school in some cases, while others will certainly need much special educational support.

Acknowledgments

The support of the Joseph Rowntree Memorial Trust for the first five years of the study and of the Department of Health and Social Security more recently is gratefully acknowledged. We are particularly indebted to our colleagues in the study for the great amount of work they put into it and for their unfailing enthusiasm.

14

The teacher and the handicapped child

D. N. Thomas

The problems of 'teaching the teachers' about the child with
a handicap are almost identical with the problems of preparing a short paper of this description — just where does one
begin? Inevitably it seems, one is forced into making vast
generalisations in the interests of brevity, knowing full well
that such procedures can be misleading, if not downright
dangerous, for all concerned — not least for those children
in whom our interests lie.

The child with special learning difficulties has, in recent
years, become the subject of numerous conferences, conven-
tions, books and articles. It is not surprising to find some
confusion amongst conscientious teachers striving for success
within the classroom, when they turn to the literature for
advice — for such literature tends to indicate not so much the
volume of new information available but rather the intensity
of the search for new information throughout the world.

Source books on special education have tended to stress
the handicaps, disabilities and limitations of handicapped
children. The result of this emphasis has been a negative
rather than a positive attitude toward their education.
Perhaps one of the reasons why we do not often collect the
most relevant information about the child is because we are
too pre-occupied with his handicap or deviant behaviour.
Professor Gunnar Dybwad offered an example of what may

happen when he said:

> In country after country, all that needed to be known was
> that there was mongolism [present] and immediately one
> knew 'they can't learn to read or write, they can't work a
> full day, they can't do this, they can't do that — and,
> because they couldn't learn we naturally didn't teach them.
> Because we didn't teach them, naturally they didn't learn'
> . . . thus went the vicious circle ('Education for the
> ineducable — an international paradox', *Forward Trends*,
> 1967,11).

Too frequently the handicap has been the facet of the child's
life by which he has become known to his teachers, to his
friends, and even to his parents. Perhaps we have carried this
preoccupation into our teaching (and our teacher training)
and failed to see the behaviours that are constructively
relevant to the learning processes. Putting it another way, if
we know more about those things that the child cannot do
than those things he might well be able to do, we are not
likely to decide the best teaching (or training) programme for
the individual child.

Such are the effects of 'labels'. It is the teacher's trade to
consider the needs of the 'whole' child — not merely that part
of him which appears to confirm the label which has enabled
him to be 'classified' or 'categorised' in some way.

Understanding the handicapped child means first understanding him as a child — and only then understanding the
ways in which his disabilities may influence his development
and behaviour. The basic motivations for affection, acceptance and approval exist whether the IQ is 50 or 150; whether
the body is beautiful or a caricature; whether the movements
are graceful or made awkward and inco-ordinate by disease or
accident, or whether the speech is melodious or guttural. The
handicapped child, like any other child, can be comfortable
and secure when he feels that he is accepted, appreciated and

liked. He will be equally uneasy and insecure when he feels rejected.

Of course, children with learning difficulties present special challenges to the teacher because, whether or not such children are grouped for instruction, each has learning abilities which require individual planning and special 'remedial' procedures. Norms cannot substitute for knowledge and experience in dealing with learning disorders. However, as Dr Mary Cleugh has said: 'in the last analysis, special educational treatment depends not on policy and organisation but on the human qualities of the teachers' (*The Slow Learner*, Methuen, 1968).

Research, particularly in this past decade, has improved methods and instruments for diagnosing and assessing learning difficulties in children and this, in turn, has increased the ability of the psychologists and physicians to determine the existence and extent of disability. Continuous development and refinement of prosthetic devices for children with physical impairments have made it possible for these children to utilise more fully the abilities they possess in spite of their handicap. Indeed, coincident with these advances in practices, the philosophy of educators and others concerning the educational placement of handicapped children has evolved toward a policy of integration within the so-called 'ordinary' school.

But at the vital, basic level, in the classroom where, if you will pardon the expression, 'it all happens', are the teachers possessed of those qualities to which Dr Cleugh was referring, particularly with regard to their attitudes toward those handicapped children who may be present in their group? Nearly thirty years ago Baruch demonstrated that student teachers who have been able to achieve a better understanding of themselves can accept in a more positive way children who display deviant behaviour patterns (D.W. Baruch, 'Procedures in training to prevent and reduce mental hygiene problems', *Journal of Genetic Psychology*, 1945, 67). Apparently, well adjusted teachers are able to enhance the personal adjustment of the pupils whom they teach — would we disagree?

Increasing the level of knowledge that teachers have concerning children with learning difficulties can be accomplished
more readily than inducing teachers to come face-to-face with
their own personalities. Providing an inter-personal setting in
which teachers can come to grips with their own needs,
conflicts and attitudes requires very careful consideration.
Dare I presume that the training of well adjusted teachers
requires well adjusted staff in colleges of education and other
institutes and schools of education? Consider the colleges of
education in England and Wales, where, after all, the majority
of new entrants to the teaching profession are trained. Given
the multiple and conflicting demands upon them from three
major partners — the Department of Education and Science,
the providing bodies (local education authorities and
voluntary), and the universities — to whom are they ultimately responsible? Indeed, what are they ultimately responsible
for?

There is no clear answer to the first question, and dissatis-
faction on the part of some of the partners who feel a
legitimate interest in the work of the colleges is guaranteed.
To say that they must produce young teachers adequate to
the needs of the schools is to speak at a level of abstraction
which has no meaningful practical application. There are
more than 33,000 schools in England and Wales and their
needs vary considerably. Furthermore they are organised in a
variety of ways by the authorities which are responsible for
them. Pre-service initial training, no matter how good, can
never confidently predict what a young teacher will face in
his or her first appointment and so necessarily equip the
student accordingly.

To the second question — what are the colleges ultimately
responsible for? — is there any answer at all? If the colleges
are held responsible for initiating educational innovation and
advance, they will be using as agents the most inexperienced
members of the profession — with predictable results. If they

exercise no leadership in this field they will be rightly criti-
cised for being reactionary and unprogressive. If they
compromise, they will be accused of timidity. Does this
make for well adjusted staff, I wonder? Or well adjusted
trainee teachers?

Conine, in sampling teachers in a mid-western American
city (significantly, only half of a randomly selected 1,000
responded to the questionnaire) showed a degree of acceptance of the disabled similar to that of the general public
(T.A. Conine, 'Acceptance or rejection of disabled persons by
teachers', *Journal of School Health*, 1969, 39, 4). Are we
happy with that? Sex was the only variable significantly
affecting attitudes, women teachers being more favourable to
the disabled than men. Conine further points out the
importance of changing teachers' attitudes, if those of the
public are to be changed.

What of attitude change? A substantial amount of research
is available which relates to the modification of attitude and
attitude measurement. The major portion of such research
appears to be in areas of socio-economic status, race and
religious prejudices. Published research dealing with the
attitudes of teachers toward children with learning difficulties
and/or handicaps is, frankly, negligible. It is assumed that if,
through certain educational techniques, one can modify the
attitudes of teachers toward a realistic acceptance of children
with handicaps, these attitudes of acceptance on the part of
the teachers will also influence children in the direction of
realistic acceptance.

The most widely used methods for the modification of
attitudes are films, group discussions, visitations, lectures,
reading materials — or any combination of these. Some
researchers have concluded that one method is more effective
than another. However, the evidence is not conclusive enough
to suggest any one technique for all situations. Haring et al.
report that teachers presented with formal lectures supported
by 'permissive' discussion sessions, films and visits to class-

rooms in which 'exceptional' children were being educated increased their knowledge concerning 'exceptional' children irrespective of their having direct experiences with the children. However, 'increased knowledge per se was not found to be a significant factor in effecting modifications of teachers' attitudes toward "exceptional" children' (G. Haring, G.C. Stern and W.M. Cruickshank, *Attitudes of Educators towards Exceptional Children*, Syracuse University Press, 1958).

From the reactions of those teachers who had few opportunities for actual experiences with 'exceptional' children, it appears that the threat of having to modify behaviour is more anxiety-producing than the real process of change itself. Introspection into how one might feel when asked to teach a handicapped child, without having a first-hand acquaintance with that child, tends to elicit rejection rather than acceptance. The confusion of fantasied imaginary conflicts, associated with anxieties stemming from anticipation of the unknown, is very difficult to resolve. Abstractions presented through 'workshops' or other programmes designed to modify attitudes are more effective as adjuncts to experience than as substitutes for experience. Seemingly, the most effective results are obtained when programmes designed for implementing attitude changes are presented in conjunction with actual experiences.

At the 'initial training' or 'pre-service' level, findings suggest that broad orientation courses are effective in increasing the information students have about children with learning difficulties. However, student numbers tend to make it extremely difficult to encourage actual teaching experience with such children, thus aiding attitudes of acceptance. In this situation, the choice of the information to communicate becomes an important aspect of attitude-change strategy.

It should not be implied that any communication will have the desired effect. Messages must actually contain information — understandable statements about factual or potentially factual matters. Too often I am afraid many 'messages' contain little or no information. Instead, they

1 say little that people can understand (the medical model),
2 ask questions rather than give answers (the academic model),
3 'destroy' what information people may have rather than provide new information, or
4 make exhortative appeals for people to develop better attitudes.

Much of the information currently given to the public via the media follows this pattern, for example, telling people that one in nine (or so) persons will require treatment in a mental hospital in their lifetime. This may very well raise anxiety, but does not help to deal with the problem, and to have said in the past 'one "spastic" child is born every eight hours' may have served a similar function.

A positive approach is required at initial training level — not the negativistic attitude referred to earlier in this paper. Too often in the past the handicapped child has become a stereotype in the teacher's mind: 'because he is . . . therefore he will. . .' and so on. The factual content of the information provided is important largely to the extent in which it induces a proper emotional state in the listener. The message should make the listener feel secure by sounding certain, by offering solutions (to classroom situations), by presenting explanations that are understandable and by reducing anxiety in other ways.

I suspect that I am in a fortunate position. As tutor/organiser of a one-year, full-time, in-service course for experienced teachers in the education of handicapped children, I have been able to bring the practitioners face to face, in small group seminar situations, with second- and third-year students in initial training. The students attend my lead lectures — in that dreadful mass-lecture form — but are subsequently able to discuss problems with qualified teachers (who are, temporarily, students) in an informal manner. The indications are that these sessions are mutually satisfying and the 'feed-back' is encouraging, at both initial and in-service training level.

It has been clear for some time that the preparation of teachers for work with children with learning difficulties cannot be met only by a relatively small number of one-year courses, such as my own in Leicester. Apart from the fact that one-year courses cannot train enough teachers, nor train them early enough in their career, it is necessary to provide, as the James Report (*Teacher Education and Training*, HMSO, 1972) recognised, special training at each stage or cycle of training. Much good would follow from a general introduction to children with difficulties in the initial, pre-service years of training, at an 'inspirational' level; more would follow if the professional guidance in the vital 'induction' year were well organised and effective, for, at this stage, support and guidance can be provided in conjunction with actual experience. But the greatest potentialities for the development of special training lies in the in-service training approach when, in the words of Lord Annan, the opportunity can be provided 'to retread the tyres of the mind' (N. Annan, 'What are universities for, anyway?', BBC TV Dimbleby Lecture, reprinted in *Listener*, 88, 2275).

One final thought, a direct quotation in fact:

Any class of young persons marked by an infirmity . . . depend more than ordinary persons do for their happiness and for their support, upon the ties of kindred, of friendship and of neighbourhood. All these, therefore, ought to be nourished and strengthened during childhood and youth — for it is then, and then only, that they take such deep root as to become strong and life lasting. . . . Beware how you needlessly sever any of these ties . . . lest you make a homeless man, a wanderer and a stranger. If the fields were all clear, and no buildings provided, there should be built only a building for schoolrooms . . . music rooms and workshop — and these should be in or near the centre of a dense population. For other purposes, ordinary houses would suffice.

The speaker: Samuel Howe
The date: 1866

15

The multi-handicapped child in a boarding school for cerebral palsy

R. A. Pedder

I should like to make a few general observations on the question of integration of the handicapped before dealing specifically with the main theme of this paper.

The Department of Education and Science issued a Circular No. 4/73 in March 1973, which contained the following passage:

> Increasing efforts are being made to devise ways of catering for less severely handicapped children in primary and secondary schools and it is generally accepted that handicapped children should not be placed in special schools if the specialised help they need can be provided in ordinary schools.

On the face of it, the above-quoted statement would appear to be quite an advance for the minimally handicapped, but we must not be misled by it, or read into it more than it contains, and assume that because a boy or girl is placed in an ordinary school all their 'real' needs are being met and the specialised help is being provided.

In this country, there has been a growing number of units for some minimally handicapped pupils in ordinary schools — particularly the partially hearing children — and one is given the impression that these are integrated situations. In fact, very many of them are not at all integrated and, apart from a limited number of school functions or assemblies, etc., these children are as isolated from the others as they ever were, except possibly by the location. Often there is no real association between the pupils in class, in the playgrounds, on the sports fields or in the important social situations.

The majority of these special units or classes are in the primary schools — where usually there is a more tolerant attitude from both staff and pupils — and it is quite significant that at the crucial time for development the system appears to break down. There is no evidence whatsoever that the more tolerant attitude of both teachers and pupils in primary schools is of any help at all, and in fact the kindly or indulgent attitudes may be quite contrary to what is really required for the child's realistic development.

An unfortunate aspect of this effort to include the less severely handicapped in the ordinary situation is the apparent lack of complete diagnosis of the child and its difficulties, or an appraisal of whether the child can cope sufficiently adequately in such an environment, with teachers who may not have had the training and/or experience to deal with these special groups of children.

It is not just a question of whether the boy or girl can get to and from school, can climb stairs or sit in class, but whether the nature of the handicap allows it to be adequately dealt with and involved in all the social, physical and other activities of the school — assuming, of course, that he or she may wish to participate.

There is also the question of whether the more obvious disability is in fact the sum total of the child's difficulties. A child with a handicap is obviously more vulnerable to other handicapping conditions which may be far more serious in preventing active participation than the more obvious handicap. A typical example that one finds is with some minimally handicapped cerebral palsied children, whose obvious physical involvement is often quite secondary to the learning problems and may involve sensory input, visual and perceptual difficulties, limited power of concentration, lack of confidence, speech difficulties, etc., etc. Yet, these children are simply considered to be slightly physically handicapped and, in due time, because of their inability to cope, can become quite severely retarded, considerably adding to their problems.

It is unfortunate, but I think the number of children referred to special schools for the cerebral palsied at the secondary stage as unable to cope, or as school failures, is as many as those referred by the schools for the physically handicapped as being in need of more specialist attention. Too often, one hears reports of children being unable to participate in sports and games, drama, physical education and other activities, including school journeys, expeditions, etc. because they have a physical handicap which prevents them from 'keeping up' with the others or because they present some-what of a problem. This means, in effect, that these young people are being denied opportunities for development, of being exposed to experiences and of active participation so that their whole school programme is being restricted and no real alternative is being provided. As a result of this, these less-severely handicapped pupils often become the passive bystanders or non-participants — not from choice, but because of 'circumstances'.

The inclusion of the less-severely handicapped in an ordinary school should not therefore be just a question of whether the school can 'contain' such pupil or pupils, but whether it, as a community, can adequately supply the needs of those pupils in what we regard as the basic elements for development and their exposure to the essential experiences of life and living for a full and satisfying future.

What, unfortunately, we are still tending to do is to separate the school from out-of-school functions. The Department's Circular will doubtless do much, one hopes, to improve the attention given to the less-severely handicapped in ordinary schools, but this is only a part of the child's life and we need to pay far more attention to what happens to these children when not in school. Do they, or can they, have the same breadth of experience of all kinds to show the 'integration' out of school that is being attempted in school?

Has any effort ever been made to evaluate the attitude and behaviour of the ordinary pupils to the handicapped within their school? At the infant or primary levels this may not be presented as a problem and the life of the handicapped child may not be unduly difficult. In fact, it may be too easy, but at the senior level the position is often very different. Are we to assume that because the school is 'containing' the handicapped there are no problems? Does the senior school boy or girl suddenly become a 'paragon of virtue' because there happen to be some handicapped pupils in their midst or are the handicapped considered odd, inferior or different, and, at best, ignored, or are they even subjected to taunts and ridicule?

We know from the statistics that there are many more handicapped children contained in infant primary schools than in senior schools. Have we examined the effect these transfers out of the ordinary system have upon these young people? It would seem that at the time when the whole question of their integration should be becoming more essential and established, they are removed to special schools. I have had quite a few of such transfers and have generally found them to be:

1   more retarded than one would have thought necessary;
2   lacking in self-confidence and social competence; and
3   physically less competent and less mobile than would have been reasonably expected, with some having developed contractions and deformities.

Even some special schools, whether they be day or boarding — and here I am concerned with those dealing with the physi-cally handicapped — often fall short of providing the experiences and opportunities that should be available. This may or may not be the fault of the school, but we should

146

look very critically at what is happening and what provision is being made.

The lives of some pupils in day schools (even for the physically handicapped) are so very restricted it is no wonder that all kinds of secondary problems arise. There are children whose world is almost entirely confined to being collected for school each day and being delivered back home each evening, where they remain — awaiting the next trip to school. The forms of activities during out-of-school hours are dependent upon the parents, most of whom (because they have little or no contact with the school and no guidance or training regarding what is required) are inclined to take the line of least resistance and depend on television viewing or other passive activity. We cannot, and must not, blame them for this, but it is hardly an edifying experience for growing youngsters.

There are, of course, those parents, probably in the minority, with the odds weighted heavily against them, who manage to give their handicapped child a very full and enriched life. However, the demands on them are extremely heavy and the price they pay can be very costly to their own physical and mental well-being, as well as to that of the other siblings and members of the family.

This extremely restricted or virtually non-existent social life and lack of exposure to the wide variety of places, people and happenings of all kinds leaves the handicapped child lacking in mental and physical stimulation and does absolutely nothing towards improving the quality of his life. There is no doubt that the children whose handicaps are more severe or more complicated are likely to cause the greatest problems, and are, in all probability, the most vulnerable. This type of very restricted life is to their ultimate disadvantage.

A handicapped person, particularly the cerebral palsied, whether in an ordinary school, a day special school, or a boarding special school should, in spite of difficulties, be a full and participating member of that community.

147

Unfortunately, one finds all too often that the cerebral palsied (especially the spastic types) who need much physical stimulation and activity are permitted to be physically inactive and often confined to a sitting position posturally disastrous to them. What kind of evidence can we obtain that the real needs of each category of physical handicap can, in fact, be provided in essentially non-specialised situations?

I well remember the earlier demands that the cerebral palsied, in particular, needed different forms of attention, both physical and education, from most other forms of physical defect. Is there any evidence that this is not now the case, or is it that the social movement towards comprehensive or integrated schooling is not taking into account the vital differences in needs that exist, and the importance of providing the essential highly skilled attention required?

I would now like to turn attention to the multi-handicapped cerebral palsied child. Unfortunately, there is a tendency amongst many people — educationalists, doctors, etc. — to refer to the cerebral palsied as if they were the victims of a simple, single handicapping condition. It is more likely that the majority of the cerebral palsied are, in fact, multi-handicapped — in many and various ways, with very different degrees of severity in each aspect of the handicap.

Statistics on these matters vary quite enormously and, in any case, are far from satisfactory or complete. Often, for educational purposes, the cerebral palsied are lumped together with the physically handicapped — certainly this applies to the Department of Education and Science classification — in a rather simple diagnostic manner or, as is written in the Department's Circular 4/73, 'Brain damage may give rise to spasticity, a speech disorder and mental retardation'. Of course, they are right — it might do just that — and it might also include visual and hearing defects, athetosis, emotional disturbance, maladjustment, perceptual disorders and practically every other learning disorder of which we have any knowledge.

The combination of the various difficulties and the necessity to give specific attention to each and every aspect of development makes it almost imperative for the child to be in a situation where the skills, experience and understanding of a highly qualified staff are available. For a variety of reasons — be they social (for example, inability of the family to cope because of other pressures, family sickness, social inadequacy, broken marriages, etc.) or because of lack of adequate facilities near the home location — many multi-handicapped children find their way to boarding special schools. Sometimes, of course, the multi-handicapped child is considered for a special boarding school because it is possibly the only place, at a given point in time, that is considered right and proper for the child to be for its future development.

Discussion regarding the placement of multi-handicapped cerebral palsied pupils in special boarding schools is often of a very emotive nature. Naturally, we are concerned that these multi-handicapped cerebral palsied children need the special boarding school and the immediate effect, emotionally, that this has on the child and its family, but I venture to suggest that so long as careful preparation and planning has been made the effect is more likely to be short- rather than long-term. Surely we would all wish that the need did not exist, but it does, and we must therefore make our decisions collectively based upon the realities of the situation and our understanding of what is best for the child and its future. If we are right in our analysis of the position that the child's future depends upon a complete developmental programme covering the whole day, how are we to achieve this unless the opportunity exists for operating the complete programme?

It seems to me that much more careful consideration should be given by the decision-makers to what the real needs of the child and its future are. If we are serious in making the statement that every individual has the right to a full life, then the over-riding factor must be 'what then is best for that person at any given point of time in its development? ' and one must ask whether the child in a special boarding school can be given all the vital ingredients for the development of the maximum independence and the provision of the experiences likely to be required for a full and satisfactory life.

However well intentioned, it is virtually impossible for the home circumstances to make this provision, some of the reasons being:

1 the natural tendency for parents to do more for their multi-handicapped child than is good for it;

2 the difficulty of providing the wide range of purposeful activities as a continuing and regular process because of the enormous strain imposed upon the parents and indeed the whole family;

3 the permitting of the opportunity of the multi-handicapped youngster to experiment in physical, educational and social situations because the family considerations make this virtually impossible;

4 the difficulty that would be experienced in exposing the child to the wide variety of experiences, outside the home, according to its age and stage of development, and

5 the problem of providing the opportunity for the necessary relationships to develop between the child and other children. Non-handicapped young people have a tendency to deal quite differently with the multi-handicapped youngster and invariably make such allowances for it that a completely unrealistic and indulgent relationship develops.

There are, quite naturally, certain disadvantages in the multi-handicapped cerebral palsied children being in special boarding schools, but I think, on balance, the advantages outweigh the disadvantages and this is reflected in the attitude of both parents and children when they have had time to come to terms with the situation.

How can the special boarding school assist in the complete 'acceptance' by the public — as a prelude to integration within society? The school should become a focal point around which many groups of people can function — not a separate or isolated community — so that ever-widening groups of people from all walks of life and with a wide variety of interests can be utilised in the interests of its pupils. The kind of groups one can and should attract are numerous.

First, there is the school staff which would normally be the teachers, therapists and houseparents or care staff who should be the basic group around which all others can function. In addition there are the ancillary staff of cleaners, drivers, cooks, etc. who have their role to play.

Second, the parents and families should be given every encouragement to be involved in school activities, so that they are not made to feel like 'outsiders' in the situation involving their child. In fact, every opportunity must be given for parents and families to play a full role in what is taking place with their own and other children. If good guidance is given to the parents and families by the school staff, the holiday periods could become much more positive and helpful. There should be frequent opportunities for the parents and children to be together both inside and outside the school so that there is no possibility of estrangement between the child and its family.

Third, the groups of people, young or old, especially interested in a particular type of activity in which one would like pupils to be involved, and which exposes them to experiences which may have some effect on their development and enrichment of life. The nature of such groups can vary quite considerably and they cross every age, social and cultural barrier in society. The 'county types' for horse riding, the fishermen and railway workers, the artists and artisans, the students in colleges and pupils in schools, the voluntary workers from all kinds of organisations, many of whom are anxious to be involved if given the opportunity and are shown what to do and how to deal with the situation. Such groups can cover an extraordinary range of activities and interests of a physical, intellectual or social nature. If we look around it is

151

quite amazing the number of groups or societies of people banded together for specific types of activities and interests.

The special boarding schools are presented with a magnificent opportunity for interesting such groups in the work of the school by exploiting those interests for the benefit of pupils. This would increase the variety of experiences to which the pupils can be exposed, which may be stimulating either physically or mentally, according to its nature, and can provide short-term interests or long-lasting hobbies and involvements.

In addition to the value such people and groups can be to our pupils, this is not entirely a one-sided exercise, as I am sure the quality of life of such people can be enriched by this association. The involvement of members of the public within the school and, probably because of it, encourages the involvement of the pupils with the public outside the school at all kinds of social, sports or cultural events. The possibilities of such involvement are enormous and arise from our desire to be outward-looking in providing pupils with a tremendous breadth of experiences.

It would seem that there are advantages to the pupils in being trained together in these various forms of social situations and, for their sakes as well as those of their parents and relatives, of being members of a group within a boarding situation according to their own age and level of intelligence. This does not mean 'isolation' but rather greater involvement in society, deriving comfort and strength from each other and eventually, one hopes, the building up of self-confidence, personal assurance and social competence. For the adults or people dealing with the pupils in these situations one finds, as a result of the development of common interests, there is less embarrassment and self-consciousness and a more natural and realistic relationship.

We can help to improve the public image of such handicapped children by:

1   ensuring that they are as socially acceptable in appearance and attitude as is possible;
2   presenting them in any situation which shows their strengths and minimises their weaknesses; and
3   making sure that they are well primed and conversant with the nature of the function, event or circumstances at which they will be present.

The regularity and consistency with which we involve the pupils in all kinds of activities outside the school — and the careful counselling which we give the people who are handling them — will, in the long run, cause the public to be less apprehensive and more ready to accept.

There are quite a number of important factors to be borne in mind when we are involving the public in activities inside and outside the school.

1   They should be counselled in how to deal with and relate to the pupils. Generally they are inclined to be 'easy' and not expect any standard, so they must be made aware of what to expect and ensure that they obtain such standard.
2   They tend to fail to correct when correction is necessary — and they need to know that correction is a necessary part of training.
3   There is a tendency to treat the pupils as more immature and they are usually more indulgent than is necessary and so give more help than is required.
4   They need counselling on what response to expect in the way of speech and to gain experience and understanding of those with difficult articulation.

In dealing with these extensions to school activities, we must not necessarily think only in terms of active participation — however desirable this may be — but also of the pupils who, because of the severity of their disability, may not be able to take part in an activity, but for whom the subject would certainly be a more enjoyable experience if one had some knowledge of, for example, car mechanics — and even more enjoyable if car rally enthusiasts are involved with the pupils and it is not necessarily left to members of staff who may not really be interested. This analogy can be read into a vast number of activities, expeditions and interests.

The special boarding school for the multi-handicapped cerebral palsied can play a great part in establishing this understanding by seeing itself as a focal point from which its pupils can be brought or taken into a variety of wider communities for all types of involvements and participation. It can also be a centre in which members of the public can play an active and purposeful role by giving to the pupils the benefits of their special interests, activities or skills, both inside and outside of the school, with all its social advantages, thereby increasing the number of people involved in serving the interests of the pupils and assisting in their development towards participation in a full and purposeful life.

The development from the close-knit family group to eventual integration in society is a gradual process for any child. This development for the multi-handicapped is probably an even more gradual process and the boarding school may well be a vital link in bridging the gaps very effectively if careful attention is paid to the need. The school should be an admirable place for constantly enlarging the horizons of the children so that, when the time arrives for them to leave, they will be far more capable of making more secure and mature relationships to meet their own particular needs — whatever they may be.

16

The special school as a normalising agency

D. Braybrook

I am basing my comments and opinions concerning integration on personal experience, so I feel I must begin by defining my experience and also the children concerned. I have worked for the past seven years in a special school that caters for deaf children between the ages of 11 and 17. All of the children were born profoundly deaf or became profoundly deaf in the first few months of life. Prior to their arrival at the school, the children had been educated in one of four different ways:

1   in a junior school for deaf children;
2   in a school for partially hearing children;
3   in a unit for partially hearing children; or
4   in a normal hearing school

They are admitted with considerably varying abilities and standards. At one extreme there are children who, at the age of 11, have no recordable reading age and who experience considerable difficulty with speech and lip-reading. At the other extreme there are those children with reading ages of 8 or 9 who are well prepared for a secondary programme. They have good speech and lip-reading and they may have possibly just failed to gain a place by selective examination at the Mary Hare Grammar School for the Deaf at Newbury, Berkshire. Whatever their achievements are upon entry, the children are essentially normal — their handicap, apart from certain other minimal additional ones, is a single handicap,

that of profound deafness. This paper is therefore concerned
solely with the education of deaf children. I hope that some
of it might apply to the education of other handicapped
children.

I am well aware that many people, with considerable justification, claim that placement in a special school is incompatible
with integration. I maintain, however, that the right kind of
special school, and the weekly boarding special school in
particular, can be an effective normalising agency that will
allow its pupils upon leaving to live and integrate in a hearing
world. Again, I am afraid I must return to definitions and
define the sort of special school I have in mind. It is essentially, if in terms contradictory, a 'normal' special school.
First, and of prime importance, the school must employ a
'natural' normal means of communication. The children must
develop an oral, as opposed to a manual means of communication. In a 'normal' special school oral education must mean
what it says: there can be no place for unnatural methods
such as finger spelling, cued speech or singing, however
systematic. It is fanciful to talk of special education as
preparing the deaf child to take his place in a hearing world
if the educational provision is based on providing innumerable props and unnatural concessions from the earliest
formative years. If we employ such unnatural approaches we
establish attitudes of complacency and acceptance in the
children and they ultimately lack true learning incentive,
inspiration and motivation. However, a special school can be
a centre where deaf children go to be specially helped to do
naturally what comes naturally to a hearing child. The
special school alone has the organisation to muster a force
of people, within and without the school, all of whom can
pursue a common purpose to make it a power house where
normal influences and examples are generated — normal
influences and examples designed to establish normal patterns
of communication and behaviour and much nearer normal
standards of achievement. Remembering that the 'natural'

oral approach is essential, I will provide more details of the sort of special school I have in mind, in order to show how the deaf child can be helped to arrive, by the age of 16 or 17, at a point where true integration is possible. The point where the young person is confident, not only in his or her ability but in himself or herself as a person. The point where they are convinced, and are capable of convincing others, that they have something to offer — not just a trade or a talent — but the full and confident personality of one who is capable not only of earning a living, but of being a full and active member of society.

I mentioned a weekly boarding school as being of special importance. One of the objections to special schools is that they isolate the child from the family in particular and from society in general. If the child travels home weekly, home is rightly held as a place of prime importance in the child's mind and yet the child gains independence from leading his own life from Monday to Friday and from travelling by himself on Friday and Sunday. The children are delighted to leave for home on Friday but they are equally delighted to return to school on the Sunday. The correct balance between home and school is therefore maintained by weekly boarding. The parents are able to appreciate and exercise their responsibilities, but the child is able to develop and become independent away from the over-protective or socially inadequate or comfortable middle-class home. When the child begins to feel independent it is necessary to help him to feel successful in his own right. Therefore, just as the oral method is an essential part of the philosophy of the school, the concept of bringing success to every child is also an essential aim. The methods of bringing success are the normal ones employed in normal schools. Perhaps the methods are used more frequently and brought into action over smaller achievements, but they are nevertheless normal ones. As teachers we are all concerned with the trivial: with M—'s sore finger, with P—'s questionable arithmetic, with D—'s dead goldfish. Yet we know only too well that in subjects, as well as in personal relationships, success brings forth greater success and that all situations must be exploited to bring positive, useful and successful learning situations.

The structure and organisation of the school is, as far as possible, like that of any normal secondary modern school. There are Prefects, Monitors, House Captains, Reports, Yearly Exams, CSE Examinations, Open Days, Sports Days and educational visits. The children are able to compare their school in considerable detail with those of their hearing friends or hearing brothers and sisters. The examinations they sit, the television programmes they watch, the uniforms they wear, the moans and grumbles they have about school, are common experiences they share with hearing children. They grow up and begin to see the world in some sort of perspective, like their hearing peers and like we did, by discussing, grumbling and laughing about them. The school is, dare I mention it, streamed throughout into an A and B stream. The range of ability covered by the two streams is, as assessed by non-verbal IQ tests, between an IQ of 56 and 138. The A children are more orally able children who will eventually take, and it is hoped secure, five, six or seven CSE passes. Their course is mainly an academic one. The B stream work is, in the beginning, somewhat similar to that of the A classes, but there is much more stress made on providing them with a good and useful means of communication. Some of the B children will achieve passes in the more practical CSE subjects at the end of their school career. Of course, the opportunities for social success, such as gaining Prefect status, House Captain status, etc., are equal in both streams. The streams exist in order to provide small, homogeneous groups of children whose language requirements are approximately the same. Our aim is therefore, as far as possible, to achieve normal standards. Only by aiming for, and we hope sometimes achieving, normal standards can we hope that true integration

will be a possibility when the children leave school. If the aim
of special education is normal standards, environment and
methods must be as near normal as we can make them.
Special education should mean that we are going to take
special steps to see that they are, rather than eternally searching
for ways and means of getting down to work of a lower level.

What of the end result? What about employment? What
about integration? I think, the best way of answering these
questions is to give information about the examination passes
gained, the employment secured and details of the recent
follow-up carried out by the Careers Officer of the Surrey
County Council, as shown in Table 16.1. Tables 16.2 and
16.3 show the range of employment taken by previous pupils
of the school.

Each year two reunions are held at the school and old
pupils return with their friends, husbands or wives, and some
very proudly return with their children. They are, I submit,
as happy and as useful a citizen as you or I. There are, of
course, those who find life difficult, there are those who make
life difficult, but these two categories are not the sole
prerogative of the deaf. I am not suggesting special school
placement for all deaf children. What I am suggesting is that
in the wide educational provision for deaf children the special
school has a vital part to play. For the profoundly deaf child
the special school can be the normalising agency that allows
him or her to be reasonably successful in achieving normal
school standards, so that upon leaving school the prospects
of employment and success in life are those of his or her
hearing peers.

D. Braybrook

Table 16.1

Name	No. of CSE passes	Employment	Follow-up comment
R—	7	Trainee draughtsman.	Settled in well, producing a good standard of work
C—	1	Working for local council	Seems happy in his work
H—	6	Warehouseman	Has successfully completed six months trial
P—	6	Drawing office clerk	Progress fair
S—	2	Sewing machinist	Working satisfactorily
J—	5	Copy typist	Happy at work
M—	2	Copy typist	Finds it difficult to adjust to working environment. Has settled fairly well
J—	2	Copy typist	Satisfactory progress
J—	6	Copy typist	Very happy
L—	2	Copy typist	Has settled and is happy at work
J—	1	Attending a further education course for the deaf	
A—		Left before CSE, attending a college of further education	
P—		Left before CSE, working in a laundry, no follow-up information	
L—	1	Works in hospital packing department	Seems happy
A—	No CSE	Machinist. Is being specially trained by Triumph International	
J—	1	Copy typist	Firm are delighted and wish they could get more girls like her
C—	6	Copy typist	Very happy at work
A—	6	Copy typist	Doing very well indeed and is happy in her work

Table 16.2   Summary of employment (as known) held by boys from Nutfield Priory, October 1972

Joiners	18	Dustman	1
Cabinet makers	3		
		Bookbinders	6
Draughtsman	9	Printers	4
Drawing office assistant	1	Printer's assistant	1
		Linotype operator	1
Turner	1		
Fitter and turner	1	Trainee accountant	1
Fitters	2		
Sheet metal workers	2	Shoe repairer	1
Fitters and welders	2		
Blacksmiths	1	Instrument maker	1
Welder and press setter	1	Pattern maker	1
Light engineering	3	Photoprinters	3
Laminator	1	Chefs	3
Armature winder	1	Storemen	3
Assemblers of electrical equipment	2	Trainee plant attendant	1
Motor mechanics	2	Dispatch clerk at a laundry	1
Panel beaters	3		
		Typewriter mechanic	1
Paint sprayers	3		
		Silk screen printer and signwriter	1
Builder's labourers	2		
Bricklayers	2	Tailors	2
Painters and decorators	2		
Painters	2	Factory hands	19
Garden and yard fitter	1	Lorry driver	2

Table 16.3   Summary of employment (as known) held by girls from Nutfield Priory, October 1972

Machinists	4
Dress design	1*
Confectioner	1
Domestic work	1
Pottery	1
Accounts clerk	1
Clerk typist	3
Copy typists	37
Clerk	2
Machine schedule operator	1
Punch card operators	6
Duplicator operator	1
Photoprinter	1
Tracers (drawing office assistants)	2
Bookbinders	5
Printer's finisher	1
Apprentice hairdresser	1
Factory work	11
Students (full-time)	3
Housewives and mothers	35

formerly   5 machinists
            17 copy typists
           1 clerk
           1 comptometer operator*
           1 duplicator operator
           6 factory hands
           1 bookbinder
           1 laundry hand
           1 stockroom assistant
           1 window display*
of these 2 are working part-time
           1 part-time copy typist
           1 part-time car delivery driver

*Further full-time course at colleges completed after leaving school

17
Integrating handicapped children into ordinary secondary schools

C. L. Frost

The integration of handicapped with normal children can take place in varying degrees and in a variety of ways, including:

1 individual integration with normal children in their ordinary schools;
2 by placing units for handicapped children in ordinary schools;
3 by building special schools on the same sites as ordinary schools and sharing the facilities between those schools; and
4 by pupils from special schools undertaking part of their studies in ordinary schools or in colleges of further education.

The city of Sheffield has a population of 530,000 and has thirty-four comprehensive, 199 primary and twenty-four special schools. It also has fifteen special units in ordinary schools and those units together with the twenty-four special schools provide educational facilities for 2,500 children.

Several of the special schools have arrangements whereby their pupils spend part of each week in a neighbouring school and three of these schools for the educationally sub-normal children arrange for their 16-year-olds to take some lessons each week in colleges of further education. Most of this integration, by arrangement between schools, is for older children and much of it is in connection with CSE and GCE work, but one school for mentally handicapped children has an arrangement whereby some of its children spend half a day each week in a neighbouring primary school, and the children from that primary school reciprocate by spending some time with the mentally handicapped in their school.

Most of the units are for partially hearing children and by the time they reach secondary school age the children in those units are usually integrated into the normal schools for a proportion of their work. One of the units is for partially sighted children in an infant/junior school and most of the sixteen children in the unit undertake part of their work and activities with the normal children. Another unit for partially sighted children is in a comprehensive school. The children in that unit vary considerably in the amount of integration — three integrate very little but seven are almost totally integrated.

Another unit which has been operating for about four years forms a resource provision for blind children working in a normal comprehensive school. This particular form of integration is only possible where there are exceptionally good resource facilities and the children have a high degree of mobility.

In spite of these provisions for special education through schools and units, a considerable degree of integration within normal classes has arisen by arrangements made between parents and individual schools. In a survey undertaken in association with the Department of Education and Science in 1970, it was found that there were 547 children with major physical handicaps in the city's ordinary primary and secondary schools. As those arrangements have all been made between the parents and the schools, and no special facilities have been asked for, or provided by the education committee, in respect of those children. Now, however, the education committee is considering the possibility of developing integration further and is looking at the facilities which ordinary schools need in order to make such integration fully effective for the handicapped children and for the other children in the ordinary schools.

For such integration to be successful it must be so planned and serviced that handicapped children receive at least as good an education as in a separate special school, whilst at the same time their being in the ordinary school must not jeopardise the progress and well-being of the other children or place serious additional strain on the teachers. This entails far more than providing appropriate material conditions, important as such conditions are. Indeed it is essential that:

1   There should be careful selection of the children to be integrated to ensure that they can reasonably benefit by being placed in ordinary schools and that they do not need such a high degree of attention that the benefits of integration are lost. For example, it is easy to provide a welfare assistant to work with such a child, but in the process the presence of the welfare assistant may prevent the child being accepted by the ordinary children.

2   There must be a willingness on the part of every member of the staff of the school to accept the handicapped children. Moreover, they must have an understanding of the handicaps and of the problems associated with them.

3   There must be adequate supporting services for the handicapped child, including medical and care services, and in appropriate cases, for example, with blind pupils, a resource teacher and a technician, to ensure that all books are available in Braille and that 2D illustrated material is produced in 3D form, if in any way possible.

4   The school furniture needs to be considered to ensure it is suitable for the handicapped children and must be inspected regularly to ensure that no defects have arisen.

5   There must be a procedure for systematic review of the educational and social development of each handicapped

child and this must be organised in such a way that a child can be moved if necessary into a special school.

With many primary school buildings, particularly where they are built on one level, it is not too difficult to integrate some handicapped children since they usually work with the same teaching group and the same teacher throughout most of the day. In secondary education, however, the situation is far more difficult since the pupils usually move from room to room for their various lessons and may indeed move between buildings which are some distance apart in some schools. Not only does this present a movement/travelling difficulty for the handicapped child, it also means that they are meeting a whole variety of teachers and in a large school of perhaps 100 members of staff, it is virtually impossible that every teacher has even a reasonable knowledge of the handicapped children and their particular needs.

Moreover, as children reach secondary school age new problems arise and it is difficult for them to join with their normal peers in visits to many of the local amenities. For example few modern discotheques are equipped to receive handicapped children! At this stage too, as boy/girl friendships are developing, it is easy for the handicapped child to feel rejected if he or she is not able to develop such a relationship with a member of the other sex.

It is also at this stage that the normal youngsters are thinking about the careers that they are going into after leaving school, but the handicapped child is compelled to face up to some of the difficult problems of his disability. If he is in a special school then most of his peers are having to face this difficulty together, but when he is in an ordinary school and finds that friends, teachers and careers officers change from telling him of all the things he can do and tell him of the limitations caused by his handicap, then an emotional situation can very easily develop and it is vital that all members of staff are aware of this situation.

This is, therefore, essentially a matter of careful preparation of the children themselves and of the staff, and providing this has been done properly and the buildings have been adapted satisfactorily for their needs, many quite severely handicapped children can be integrated successfully into secondary schools and into colleges of further education.

18

Description of a current survey of disabled students at universities and polytechnics in Great Britain

Alan Chamberlain

Timing and history

The survey of disabled students in higher education started in the spring of 1972. The subject was first considered for a research study after contact with the Open University. The Open University accepts students for degree courses who might not be admitted to the ordinary universities or polytechnics because they do not possess the formal entrance qualifications, or because they are prevented from attending a college for some other reason. Open University students study at home by means of correspondence courses, television programmes, locally situated tutors and study centres, and by attendance at summer schools.

The teaching system is therefore particularly suited to certain categories of severely disabled students and a proportion of them have registered with the Open University. Some problems have been experienced, however, when disabled students attend study centres and summer schools. There have been problems in accommodation and in some cases special attention has had to be given to their learning needs in relation to other students. For example, at the summer schools there is a need to ensure balanced seminar groups to enable all students to participate fully and it could be disastrous for a discussion group to have a concentration of people who are deaf or have speech defects. Our talks with people from the Open University prompted us to consider the situation for disabled students at the ordinary universities and polytechnics.

The survey

Preliminary investigations showed that a number of in some cases very severely disabled people managed to gain acceptance to a degree course at university, to complete the course satisfactorily and very often to go on and do postgraduate work. We also found that the available projections indicated an increase in the size of the disabled population, due to higher post-natal survival rates and also to the increasing numbers of young people involved in motor car accidents. The tragedy of Thalidomide pointed up this trend and the Chronically Sick and Disabled Persons Act, 1970, has brought the situation to the attention of the media and the public.

During our preliminary investigations we came across people with severe disabilities who, with the advantage of degree-level education, were able to obtain and cope with high-level and responsible occupations. Statisticians, for example, can operate as well from a wheelchair as they can from an armchair. We came to the conclusion that given the right educational opportunities and support, people who are disabled could compete for certain types of job on equal terms with their non-handicapped peers, whereas without that education they might be confined to competing for jobs which would require manual dexterity or communications skills which could put them at an immediate and real disadvantage.

The disabled person's educational career starts much earlier than entry to university, but the attention of the public and the professionals is already focused to some degree on secondary education. Very little research has been done on higher education for the disabled. Our intention in this survey is to obtain base data, to focus attention and generally start the ball rolling. Our survey will be completed by the end of 1973, but at the present time I can give some indications of the areas of interest which we will be considering in our final report. I will therefore describe the scope of the research and the methods we have employed, and go on to give some examples of the types of problems which students who are disabled have told us about and some of the questions these raise.

The scope of the survey

Higher education in Britain covers certificate, diploma, and various professional courses, as well as degree work. The field is so varied and extensive that it was necessary to limit the boundaries of the subject in order to examine the question in depth while keeping within the resources and time spans available. We decided to define these boundaries by including only disabled people who were following undergraduate or postgraduate courses at universities and polytechnics in Great Britain. The assumption was that degree courses at universities and polytechnics represent the pinnacle of higher education. This enabled us to examine a population who had crude parameters in common: they were all educated to university entrance requirements; they were following full-time educational courses of comparable level and duration; and they were of a comparable age group. We also had a crude control group, which consisted of the rest of the undergraduate population, for whom there were published statistics and other information. We hoped that by selecting disabled students at universities and polytechnics we could demonstrate factors which would be significant to all disabled students in higher education whatever courses they follow.

Our first task was to provide an operational definition for the term disabled. We had several considerations in mind.

Severe disability presented few problems but the less severe and marginal conditions are more difficult to define. Added to this definition problem was the consideration of identifying the population. A person in a wheelchair is highly visible, a person who is deaf is less apparent, and there are a host of conditions which, while being disabilities, would usually pass unnoticed. In order to identify our population, once defined we were going to have to rely on the university and polytechnic authorities. With these factors in mind, we finally decided to make the operational definition as broad as possible, taking in any condition which might produce educational disadvantages, excluding only psychological conditions.

The latter were excluded partly on ethical grounds, in that interviewing a psychologically disturbed person might exacerbate the condition, partly on grounds of definition, in that psychologists, psychiatrists and medical doctors tend to disagree among themselves concerning the diagnosis of mental illness, and partly on practical grounds, because it is probable that most undergraduates at some time or other are in a condition which could be called unbalanced. This left us with a wide range of conditions which included the diabetic, the haemophiliac, the blind and the deaf, the amputee and the paralysed.

We thought that a broad definition would reduce the difficulty for the universities in deciding whether they should include or exclude a particular person. It should also allow us to examine whether in the marginal cases there are educational disadvantages and difficulties which are not generally recognised. Such broadness, however, also brings another methodological problem because in many cases the universities will be unaware of the marginal cases. Since starting the project we have indeed found that they sometimes even have difficulty in identifying students with severe disabilities. However, the result of this is that at the end of the day, we shall not be able to say that the population we have identified is the exact total of people at universities and polytechnics who have a disability. We do, however, think that the figure we produce will give a fair approximation of the total number involved, certainly so of the more visibly disabled. We shall also have a wealth of information of a qualitative nature concerning these and the less visible conditions.

In this survey we have not aimed at statistical exactitude. Our main object is to identify and highlight the range of problems which are faced, and to give examples of how these can be mitigated.

Methods

The method we employed was to send a multi-section questionnaire to each university and polytechnic in Great Britain. This was in six sections, the first four to be answered by various officers and staff of the university, such as the medical officer, careers officer and so on. The fifth section was to be filled in by the students union and the sixth by the disabled students. The universities and polytechnics were asked to distribute these sections to the various staff members and students union and to send the last section to all those students whom they could identify as having some disability. The sections were to be returned independently, and in the case of the students, anonymously if they wished.

From the returns of this questionnaire we selected a sample of institutions to carry out interviews with members of staff and with students. The criteria for selection were based on the environmental features and geographic distribution of the institutions, the number of disabled students returning questionnaires, the institution's admissions policy concerning disabled students, and whether they were polytechnics or universities. Nineteen institutions out of a total of 150 were selected in order to demonstrate the range of situations and conditions. Interviews at these institutions were carried out in February and March 1973.

Eighty per cent of the institutions returned the questionnaire and from these we have had replies from over 250 students who have a disability which falls within our definition. We asked these institutions to estimate the numbers of disabled students who were studying with them. Forty-three universities replied and estimated a total of 416 disabled students. Of the polytechnics, eighteen replied and estimated a total of 138 disabled students. This gives an estimated total population of disabled students at 80 per cent of the universities and polytechnics in Great Britain, of 554, approximately 0.2 per cent of the student population at these institutions.

Examples

These replies represent conditions varying from a student following a postgraduate course who is confined to a wheelchair and needs to be assisted in all personal functions, has a severe speech defect and can only write by means of an electric typewriter, through people with amputated limbs, students on renal dialysis, people who are blind or deaf, to students with haemophilia, dyslexia and epilepsy.

Some students who replied have pointed out that they do not consider themselves to be disabled. Typical of these is the well controlled epileptic or diabetic who by following a particular regime can participate on equal terms with other students and has often not revealed his condition to his fellows and does not feel that he is disadvantaged in any way.

Our field work and analysis is not yet complete but nevertheless we would like to suggest some questions which are already surfacing from our survey and which will probably be dealt with in our report.

The first is that even though our definition included quite marginal cases of disability, the number of disabled students is very much lower than one would statistically expect in relation to the proportion of the population who are disabled and the proportion of the population entering universities and polytechnics on degree courses.

The second interesting point is the difficulty which many institutions had in identifying their disabled students. Questions of medical ethics and personal confidentiality came into this of course, but even so it is quite clear that the administrative officers and the health officers in some cases had little idea of whether there were any disabled students at the institution.

This situation points to a divergence of opinion on how to cater for people who are disabled, or indeed for other minority groups who might require special considerations. It is the question of identifying and labelling people. We have come across some students who, although registered as disabled, refuse to display the disabled parking disc on their vehicle in order to avoid a perceived stigma. Similarly we suspect that many disabled people in the general population refuse to register as disabled, although it might be advantageous for them to do so.

From an institutional point of view, if special provision for the disabled is to be made, the individual with a disability and his needs have to be identified. On the other hand, the individual may reject such identification as a denigration of his personality, or as an infringement of privacy, or, as occurs in some cases, try to transcend an assigned role by refusing to admit the reality of the condition.

Another factor which has been indicated to us is the social acceptability of certain conditions. In particular there appears to be little stigma associated with blindness, and our preliminary impression is that blind students tend to be relatively well catered for and often appear to be militant and extrovert in communicating their needs and obtaining their rights.

One of the most interesting factors which has so far come to light is the situation of disabled students for whom special accommodation has been made available. At one university for example, arrangements were made for a student confined to a wheelchair to live in wardened accommodation connected to the university health centre. For the student this was a near disaster. Due to staffing arrangements the building was locked at a particular time each night and he had to summon the warden in order to get in. He was isolated from the main student accommodation and had little social contact with other students.

He became depressed, his academic work suffered, and there was some question of whether he should continue his undergraduate study. Due to his persistence and initiative the authorities were persuaded to allow him to live in a hall of residence during his second year. Although this building was far from ideal for a person in a wheelchair, having innumerable steps and swing doors, on moving in he immediately developed close relationships with other students, his depression vanished and his academic work improved.

This example indicates the need to consider a person with a disability as a whole person with a full range of social needs. The physical environment and special aids and care in this case were less important than the need for the individual to experience full social relationships. The question of social isolation has been raised by far more students in our survey than the question of access or aids. This may be because in order to follow an undergraduate course at all their aids and the physical access must reach some minimum level of suitability, but we shall not know this without further research.

The alternative side to this question is the disabled person's consciousness of being a burden on others. The student in this example eventually left the hall of residence to live with a few other students in a flat. While he enjoyed this and there was no friction between the group, he returned after one term to the hall of residence because he felt that his condition, whether he willed it or not, created demands on his fellows which were too much for them.

There are two aspects here: one is the effect of his perception on the disabled student — the feeling that he is a burden on his fellows may even be imaginary, but can nevertheless affect him adversely; the other is the real effect on his fellow students — the demands may in fact be too much for them. Their social life or academic work may be affected. They may become very involved with the disabled person, identifying with him to the extent that they develop a guilt feeling that they are not doing enough, or that other people are not doing enough for him. In both cases this can affect their work and play, and even lead to the need for counselling or psychological care. This phenomenon is not only applicable to students. A doctor from a university health service told us of her own involvement with a severely disabled student and the distress it caused her when the student finally had to give up her studies.

We feel that this question is especially pertinent where the institutions rely on other students to help out. I would not argue against students helping each other, quite the reverse, but I think it is necessary to bear in mind that there are also dangers in such a policy. A danger that the disabled person will feel that he is a burden, a danger that his fellow students will feel the need to give more than they are capable of without themselves suffering in some way. It must also be borne in mind in relation to this situation that we are dealing with a group of young people who are at times placed under extreme pressure as a result of their studies.

On the other hand, there are students who have conditions which pass unnoticed by their peers and in some cases, as a reaction to disclosing their condition, they limit their social interaction with other students and become 'loners'. We have had replies to the questionnaire saying that the case was marginal and caused them no difficulties but when interviewed they disclosed their restricted social life. They might be very bitter about their condition, or have reached a modus vivendi which allows them to accept their lack of social life. Whether a condition is easily revealed depends on two main factors — the personality of the individual concerned, and the social acceptability of the condition. If the former is the main factor in concealment, then an adequate counselling system at the institution might help. If it is the latter factor which promotes concealment, then I think that the solution lies in a better informed public, and of course some of the national voluntary societies have already played a major part here and will need to continue and expand this function. In practice the two factors interact and support is needed from both the sources I have mentioned. A number of students have told us how, once they have found confidence to reveal their condition to their friends, they have found that it makes no difference at all to their relationships and they themselves feel so much better for it.

The last major point which has come up so far is that most of the institutions have not seriously considered the question of disabled students at all. In a large number of cases they have told us that they deal with problems as and when they arise. That is, if they accept a disabled person on a degree course, they will then consider any special provision that is necessary. Many of these have given examples of special provision they have made in the past, and it would appear that in some places and for some students this system is quite adequate. In other places they have said that as they have never had any disabled students there has been no need to make any special provision. In a few places we have been gratified to learn that the receipt of our questionnaire has made them aware of their lack of knowledge of their own disabled students and that they are now considering the question on an institutional basis.

We do not want to paint too black a picture, because there are some institutions which are doing or plan to do a great deal, even to the extent of providing purpose-build accommodation and caring units for the severely disabled, and there are others where, although the provision is of an ad hoc nature, they go to great lengths to ensure that the student has everything he needs. One student with polio who needs sticks to walk said that he was embarrassed at the lengths the institution went to to meet his requests and had given up asking because most things were of only marginal assistance to him but involved great cost to the university.

Another student typified a theme running through many of the comments made to us that 'both the student body and the university were unseeing rather than uncaring'. I think that this might be an important distinction, especially in those places where they say they make provision as and when the need arises. Everybody would agree that the disabled person should be encouraged to view himself as a first-class citizen, with all the social rights, obligations and duties of any other citizen, while at the same time recognising the reality of his condition and limitations. He is not helped in this if he is forced into the position of the constant supplicant. 'Caring' on the part of authorities is not always sufficient, they must be 'seeing' also.

There are very simple provisions which can be made. A 21-year-old undergraduate who has defective control of his arms through polio has reported to us that he has only just tried an amanuensis and found it preferable to any other method. Why on earth was he not offered or advised to try this method before? Another student points out that there are no toilet facilities for the disabled in the reading room of the British Museum and when he wants the loo he has to trek to another part of the building. At the other extreme, where the authorities not only 'cared' but were 'seeing' also, a specially adapted cottage was made available for a student so that he could live there with his wife who helped to look after him.

A number of students have made the point that they benefited from attending ordinary schools rather than special schools. In some cases they have lived in a residential school for the handicapped but have attended classes at a local grammar school. For the blind or for the severely disabled this latter appears to be an ideal arrangement. Their physical, medical and caring needs can be catered for at the residential school for the handicapped, they benefit from mixing with the non-handicapped at the ordinary school and any extra academic help they require can be made available by the special school.

A large percentage of those who make this point have told us how they obtained entrance to an ordinary school because of pressure by their parents. In some cases a better description would be that their parents fought a very hard battle to get them accepted. One student relates that a headmistress finally capitulated on the condition that the parents bore all the responsibility for any accidents that occurred and for all transport, etc. That this child is now an undergraduate would seem adequate justification for his parents' determination. Almost all the disabled students who replied to us and whom we interviewed have emphasised the desirability for the young disabled person to mix and be educated with the non-handicapped where it is at all possible.

I have only been able to give you a description of the research and an indication of a few of the questions which have so far come to our notice. Our final report will, we hope, provide information which will help educational institutions in planning future provision, will demonstrate difficulties which students experience and ways in which these can be mitigated and give general information to people with disabilities who wish to study in the field of higher education.

Postscript

Since this paper was first presented the research described in it has been completed and published as *Disabled Students in Higher Education*, National Innovations Centre, 1974, available through Research Publications Services Ltd.

19

A philosophy for life for 16–25-year-old physically handicapped children

Marc Gicquiaud

One day the children entrusted to our care will grow up, so we must ask ourselves 'what does life hold for the cerebral palsied? ' It is our duty to prepare them for whatever does lie ahead.

The handicapped

Some twelve years ago it was the general belief that by concentrating on specialist techniques for rehabilitation and training, great improvements would occur in the handicapped child's condition. All our efforts were concentrated in producing as much progress as possible, in the hope that great physical improvements would transform his chances in future life.

Our treatment brought some improvement to the condition of the cerebral palsied and so he was able to acquire certain functional activities which, without us, it would have been impossible for him to realise. However, once handicapped he will always remain handicapped, as we have not succeeded in making such spectacular progress that he can be truly socially integrated.

Our children, having become adults, do not walk about unnoticed; they are remarked upon. This is why alongside functional rehabilitation, true education also has a very real place. It is the adaptation of the handicapped person not only in acceptance of his own handicapping condition, but also his relationship with other people that is of supreme importance.

In the light of our past experiences, we know that a young handicapped person of around 12, who can only get around with difficulty because his body is essentially non-ambulant, will ultimately abandon trying to walk as it is too difficult for him. He would rather concentrate his efforts in another field where he will make more progress, because he is able to move around more easily and quickly in a wheelchair.

In effect, what we can do is to try to improve his function from the very beginning. If the handicap is minimal then there will be spectacular progress, and even if it is severe it is still possible for a considerable amount of progress to be made. The parents will be happy for, as they know the child well, they will notice marked improvements. However, to the untutored eye, not familiar with the situation, he will still remain a person with a considerable handicapping condition that is immediately noticeable.

Here lies the key to the whole problem. Our goal is to integrate the cerebral palsied into society and we must not forget the most important thing of all — society is essentially made up of non-handicapped people. As far as the future of the cerebral palsied is concerned, it is with the rest of society that we must be preoccupied. We must try to put ourselves in their place in order to understand their faults. We must integrate ourselves into society for we are inclined to be too inward-looking as we are constantly with our handicapped children. Consequently we tend to scorn the public who react unfavourably and who reject us.

The others — the non-handicapped

This group divides itself into two parts. First, there is the group that showers pity upon the poor unfortunate little child. 'How sad it is,' they say; they give money; they rush forward to pick the child up when he falls and occasionally they receive a crack over the head with a walking stick for their pains! The second group are those who are frightened and so seek to defend themselves for fear of contamination by the handicapped person. Sometimes they are indignant that we dare show them such children. There is, in this situation, all the elements of a divorce without hope or means of reconciliation.

It is of course natural that if we are ignorant of something we are also morbidly curious. We would probably stop to look at an accident or a fire, so it is hardly surprising that adults stop to look at handicapped people who they have probably never seen before and who therefore excite their curiosity. We must know how to explain and thus teach people to become accustomed to these things. We must learn how to accept and take other people exactly as we find them.

We must teach our children and our adolescents tolerance and show them that it is they who should show pity for these people who are upset by them. They themselves should make the effort to calm them down and to make them feel secure in their company. In this way we shall adapt the handicapped to accept society.

Experience has shown us that any group will reject a weak member who lets himself be rejected. This is the person who cannot take a joke or be teased; in other words the sort of person who does not fit into a group pattern and so automatically becomes isolated. We must therefore try to prepare the cerebral palsied for society such as it is and not as it might be.

The method

This group of children must achieve a certain degree of maturity and develop a positive personality of their own. The

method of teaching must be adapted to each child, for no two
children are the same. A punishment might mean virtually
nothing to one child, but could amount to a complete catas-
trophe to another. One child will be 'a good child' without
much difficulty (it is just his natural temperament), but
another child will be disturbed. Our main task is to awaken,
arouse and develop the personality and this must be accomplished in the environment in which the individual finds
himself so that he may come to realise his own responsibility
to that situation.

It should be remembered that 'integration' is the current
mode, but it must also be remembered that this is only the
ultimate aim. To attain this end is extremely difficult. People
are not prepared for it and it is too easy to sit and wait for
other people to take action and then criticise them. Participation in a plan of integration must be achieved by deliberate
actions upon the part of everybody and it works best in an
atmosphere of security, calm and mutual trust. We must never
allow other people, especially those who are dependent upon
us, the slightest indication of uncertainty, nor must we arouse
fear in them.

In group discussions handicapped people ask a great many
questions concerning their handicap. These usually concern
the significance and meaning of words that they hear people
using, such as handicap, debility, impaired motor function,
etc. In our opinion these questions must be answered with
the utmost frankness and directness. It must be understood
that it is not their own handicap that preoccupies their minds,
but the way in which it appears to the general public. They
want to know the answer to the question 'why does everybody stare at us?'

We often have difficulty in interpreting the ideas, the
hopes and fears of the cerebral palsied to other people. On
two occasions we invited a group of people being trained as
teachers and a group of people being trained for specialist
work in various institutions to come and question some

young adolescents that we had chosen for the purpose. I was absolutely astonished by this experience. Our young people had the situation perfectly under control. They replied intelligently to the questions put to them and explained in great detail, and with great insight, their life and their problems. This is why I now believe that the integration of the cerebral palsied in society is not our job but in fact theirs.

When a cerebral palsied person is resident in a centre, every effort should be made to see that he goes out as often as possible. He will, of course, go home to his family, but he must also have as wide an experience as possible of the rest of the world, preferably through small groups. All kinds of occasions present very good opportunities for this sort of activity and each occasion where they are likely to come into contact with other people should be exploited. For example, sport can offer a great deal; our adolescents go fencing every two weeks with pupils from a nearby school.

I do not believe for a moment that a long and lasting friendship will result each time one of these occasions takes place. The forming of a relationship is a complex structure of empathy between two people which must not be forced, but at least let us facilitate as many occasions as possible where close contact can take place.

Young people who have been brought up in an atmosphere where they have been very close to our handicapped children are eventually no longer surprised or curious when they see them. It is by investing in this way in the young and future generations that the social integration of the handicapped in society will one day be realised.

Work situation

There are two essential problems which preoccupy the adolescent cerebral palsied. First, the fact that everybody stares at him and second, what is to become of him in the future? We have already considered the former. The latter is a subject about which they speak much less because this particular anxiety is a very deep-seated one. It is very often the cause of depression or aggressive behaviour around the age of 14. With all these personality and character problems we have noticed spectacular improvements from the day that our children become grown up in their own eyes. When they understand that they can remain at the Centre in a new section of it for those over 14 and especially when they have proved satisfactorily to themselves, and also to everybody else, that they can achieve something and that they will at least be able to do some form of work, the problems recede.

However, we would not be satisfied if all that is achieved is the conditioning of our adolescents to jobs which involve only simple tasks. We must also take into account their tastes, choices and aspirations. We have, therefore, set up a training programme that is divided into three stages.

The first stage is for those under 14. This is a period of work initiation. It includes getting to know and to use simple tools such as a hammer, a screw-driver, a saw, the work-bench and so on. Simple activities are chosen according to the level of function and the age of the child.

The second stage, from 14 onwards, is that of a very broadly based apprenticeship which takes place in two workshops. The boys' workshop is an agricultural one which includes livestock and the girls' centre is orientated towards housework, cooking and sewing; in other words it is domestically orientated.

In these two work areas, the adolescent learns first of all the necessary basic movements and then he progresses through as many different activities as possible. For example, sometimes he uses dangerous industrial tools such as a cutting drill, a blow-pipe, a soldering iron, an electric cutter, etc. Besides these industrial activities there are agricultural pursuits such as looking after livestock like goats, sheep and ponies. We teach them to persevere until they succeed and also to carry out menial and boring tasks — digging holes, carrying away earth, making manure heaps, etc. This teaches them about routine and helps to develop a professional conscience. For example, they must understand that animals need to be fed and looked after even on Sundays. They must learn about the constraints imposed by warning notices, learn to order goods to be delivered on a precise day, to harvest before the frost arrives, the cycle of rain, when holidays occur, etc. They must learn how to take care of animals or work-tools and to become acutely aware of everything that affects the work situation they are in. They must know, for example, that the cost of tobacco rises and falls depending on the quality of the leaves and how they dry out, etc. In ·brief, he learns all about work from as many different aspects as possible — about tiredness, keeping to time, market prices and so on.

The third stage is that of production. The adolescent is placed in the industrial workshop where he is given a position making small parts which are then incorporated in the work-line. He learns to follow a work pattern, then to settle down and improve the rhythm of it and to persevere in this mono-tonous activity for a work day of eight hours.

That, in broad outline, shows the general scheme which we have begun to use as a pattern for work training. This scheme is adapted for each adolescent. If, for example, he is a lightly handicapped person and is very good at metal-work, then his apprenticeship in this area would be pushed as far as possible along those lines, but if the person is more handicapped, it is probably better to move him more quickly into the industrial workshop and to start to condition him to a work-post which he could go on to in a sheltered workshop.

The search for future placements must be started as soon as possible. Our philosophy of teaching must be adapted as far as possible, first to the desires of the adolescent himself, and second to the type of work that it is possible to find him as future employment. It is essential that a dialogue should take place, taking into account his realistic aspirations, the possibilities of employment within his home area, and his handicap before a realistic choice can be arrived at.

Leisure activity

If we can put this type of programme into operation, we shall have gone a long way towards coping with their principal worry, namely their future. However, we must also understand that for most of the time they will be involved in very monotonous work, offering little stimulation or interest. This will enable them to earn enough money, hopefully, to keep themselves, but it certainly will not arouse any enthusiasm for a life wedded to the machine.

So, besides their work, we must be able to give them something else; something which will allow them to be happy. In other words, we must give them a philosophy for life. This is, of course, a very delicate task to undertake because it is up to individual choice and so here again our task is to try to guide and encourage them.

If we look around us at what constitutes 'joie de vivre', we will see that some people find it in love, others in religion, some when they are out fishing, others in gardening, in sport, in playing music and so on. The role of the teacher is therefore to respond to these needs and to bring them about. If our fellow countrymen are not used to the idea of the cerebral palsied getting married, and if the structure of adult social life does not yet allow for this ambition (many hostels with work centres still do not admit mixed populations), it is our duty to bring about change in order that these goals can be realised.

Some of our young people spend their leisure hours fishing on our two lakes which are well stocked with fish, while some of the others envisage making a little corner of the garden their own personal responsibility. We hope in the future to provide them with the possibility of learning how to play the pipes and drums. Whereas many of these activities take place by choice of the adolescent, we do insist that they take part in some form of sport. The sports which we cater for are archery, rifle shooting, table tennis, hand-ball, tricycle racing, javelin throwing, etc. Fencing, which we have been doing for four years, has been a great success. We have some people at the Centre who are very good. As members of the French Team for the Physically Handicapped they have taken part in matches in Belgium and Germany. For a year now we have also done horse riding and in a few months time we shall actually have four ponies of our own.

As in the work situation, success in the sporting field becomes a very important factor which helps to give balance to their character. When the handicapped person succeeds in sport it boosts his ego considerably, for he knows he can rival, and indeed surpass, the non-handicapped person who has probably never fenced or ridden a horse in his life!

The future

We prepare our adolescents for society just as it is and we hope that they will be able to integrate into the work of other people.

We do, of course, realise that the economic situation is in a continual state of flux. When the work situation is good, then a lot of contract work is available from large factories for the sheltered workshops, but at other times, during a recession, this work is not available. We know that sometimes handicapped people find great difficulty in finding employment.

We also realise that amongst our children some of them are much too severely handicapped and will never find real work. They will only be capable of a simple occupation which will be achieved only in a very slow and laborious fashion. It must also be remembered that there are even certain people who are lightly handicapped who (though able to succeed in a quite complex task) will never for one reason or another be able to find a job of work.

For those of us who are trying not to be too idealistic and more practical, it is evident that the majority of our children, because of their handicap and their limitations, will never be able to live except in a centre or in specially adapted surroundings. So we must hope that the centres do not become simply institutions shut off from the rest of the world. They must be as open as possible, as out-going as possible, and allow freedom to those from outside to visit. If, of course, the majority of our adults work in sheltered workshops, it is possible to create residential hostels away from the work situation. It is possible to integrate a small unit of handicapped people in a flat in an ordinary residential area, and it might be possible for someone who is more lightly handicapped to have rooms in the town or a youth hostel.

In reality, we know very little about what the future holds. We have very little control over its material conditions, but at the same time we must not compromise by allowing the cerebral palsied to become introspective, to draw into their shells or to make themselves 'forgotten people'. Life is there all around him and with other people, and like other people, he has his own rightful place and must be taught to hold on to it.

Conclusion

We have a group that were once children; now they are adolescents and soon they will become adults and it is for adulthood that we must prepare them — to take part in the life of those directly around them and to take part in the life of the community.

What is most important to the adolescent is that we must try to help him to resolve the mammoth problems that preoccupy his mind: the stares and the unkind words, the apprehension about his future. We must give him a goal, a meaning, a philosophy for life and help him to be as happy as possible.

Just because someone is handicapped does not necessarily mean that he is totally incapacitated. They can, and must, be involved in life in general — we must encourage them to persevere and make certain that they succeed in doing a task well, no matter how small.

We who care for the handicapped must not be seen as their masters, but as their friends. We must make ourselves worthy of their confidence in us by our sincerity and our simplicity. We must enable them to become true men and women — individuals who are understood and accepted, and who, as far as their handicap permits, can take their rightful place in the active life of the community.

Note

This chapter was translated from the French by Anita Loring.

20
The young adult and his desire for integration

E. E. Doherty

In this paper I shall base my remarks mainly on the more severely handicapped adult who is unlikely to find employment and until now has normally been in residential care — in particular on those of average or above-average intelligence and in the 18-30 age group.

The society in which we live does not make integration easy for any of us. Ideologically, it is deeply divided, with irreconcilable differences of opinion on matters of vital concern — permissiveness in sex and pornography, obscenity in the arts and the media, violence and the effect of its portrayal, crime and punishment. Economically and socially it is highly competitive, placing enormous value on economic growth, job status, promotion, wage differentials, everything that we sum up in the phrase 'the rat race', and in this area the handicapped are at a particular disadvantage. Nevertheless, it would be wrong to say 'we must wait for society to change before we can do anything about the integration of the handicapped'. This is a counsel of despair. Societies do not change overnight, and meanwhile there is much that can be done in the short term to promote our objectives.

What do we mean by 'integration' for the handicapped? In my view it has four components, all of which must be present in some degree:

1   Recognition. The handicapped person must be accorded his appropriate status, and, if he is an adult, addressed

      as an adult; not as a child or as mentally subnormal.

2   Acceptance. He must be accepted by others for what he is, without fear, anxiety or resentment and he must feel this acceptance.

3   Relationships. He must have the opportunity to make normal satisfying relationships.

4   Experience. He must have the opportunity to have normal experience, so far as is in his power.

All these components are more or less rare in the lives of very many handicapped people, and it so happens that their initial letters spell the word 'rare' — a useful aid to the memory.

The need for acceptance and recognition will be considered later. The need for satisfying relationships is perhaps the one we are in general aware of most. Much of our life centres around other people and our dealings with them, and our happiness in large measure depends on our being on easy, natural and equal terms with those around us. Few of us are self-sufficient and self-contained; we have need of friends — of a certain number of closer relationships which may begin quite casually at work or from a shared interest or activity. They only become friendship when they develop into something more; that mysterious, unanalysable sharing of affection which obeys no rules but with which we are all familiar. The handicapped need these too — if anything more than other people. Unfortunately they are at a disadvantage. Their relationships with others often begin with dependence, and an actual need for the other person's help. A dependent relationship is not, on the face of it, an ideal basis for friendship, and, of course, if it remains at the level of helper and helped and no more it is not real friendship in the usual sense. However, such links do quite often, in my experience, grow into something more which is entitled to the name of friendship. Helper and helped can get to know each other as individuals, possibly in their family backgrounds, and find in each other a shared interest, a sense of humour, a common attitude to life or some other seed-bed of liking and mutual

192

regard. In such cases the fact of handicap becomes comparatively unimportant — it should certainly not be seen as the
controlling factor which gives the relationship its quality. Too
often this mistake is made. An observer, who may know both
of the people involved only superficially, merely sees the
externals of the relationship, noting the help which is given,
and so assumes too readily that there is no more to it than
that. In any case, one may ask, how often are ordinary friendships fully equal, without some emotional dependence, some
greater need, on one side than on the other? They very often
have an aritifical origin, in that one person joins an organisation for no other reason than to make friends. This is a very
important aspect of the problem of integration, and one
which has not received the attention it deserves.

The handicapped person needs, as far as his handicap
permits, to enjoy the same experiences as his peer group of
similar background and interests. He will be deprived of some
by his physical limitations — lack of mobility, defective
speech, or lack of motor skills — although the effects of these
can be mitigated to some degree by aids and appliances, and
by improved facilities for transport. The campaign for greater
accessibility for the handicapped to public buildings has had
a fair amount of success in this country in recent years, and
shows what can be achieved. A more intractable problem is
the tendency to deprive the handicapped of normal experiences for arbitrary reasons unconnected with their handicap.
This may be out of a wish to protect them from getting hurt
or disappointed, or because the routine or convenience of
others is supposed to require it, or because it is quicker for
someone else to do tasks for them. These are understandable
attitudes, and all of us who have responsibility for the
handicapped should re-examine our own attitudes from time
to time to see how we score in this area.

The range of experiences and possibilities open even to
quite severely handicapped people has increased dramatically
in the last few years. A number of students in wheelchairs

and needing total care have been through university, and though the difficulties, for themselves and for others, have been considerable, it is likely that the rewards have been sufficient to make the effort worth while. Certainly the students themselves have no doubts about it. The Open University now offers an easier alternative option, through study at home, but the evidence so far suggests that it will be a welcome extra opportunity rather than an acceptable alternative. The University of Sussex is opening this year a new centre for handicapped students, with help available, and there are plans for a hostel on similar lines at Oxford.

New ventures, such as Habinteg which is designed to provide housing in the community for the handicapped, with help available for those who need it, is in striking contrast to the traditional concept of residential care in special institutions which has been the norm until now. It illustrates a remarkable change of mind from only a few years ago, when a handicapped person in need of help who wanted to try to live independently of institutions was told things like 'that's what they all want', or 'how are you going to pay for your helper?' These were understandable reactions when it was assumed that the handicapped would fit into the rather stereotyped and inflexible moulds created for them by a society which genuinely cared but did not consult. We are witnessing the birth of new responses; in the future, we are going to try to make our provision more flexible, to correspond with the handicapped person's own hopes and desires, and instead of saying 'it's impossible', 'how unrealistic of you', we are going to say 'How can we make it possible? How can we finance it?'

Do the handicapped want integration? Perhaps a more interesting question would be — if they don't, why don't they? There can be no doubt that for the less intelligent the demands of normality would be too great, and also for those in the older age ranges. The sad thing is that here one is talking, not of the 50-year-old and upwards but of people aged only 30 or 35 upwards, who already exhibit the settled habits and rigid responses of much older people in the normal community. I shall return to this problem later.

Where the younger handicapped person of average intelligence is concerned, however, there can be no question that they do want integration, although they may not always do very much about achieving it. At Oakwood Further Education Centre, for example, a considerable degree of integration with life outside has been achieved, but in a rather narrow field — with students at the University of Essex, with the local churches, the Labour Club, the pubs, the football team — but on the whole students have not joined local organisations or attended their meetings. There is an inward-looking tendency, and integration has tended to be an import rather than an export. Nevertheless, it is wanted. In fact, I would call it their most important need, the need on which their whole future depends. It is the prime condition for their development into mature, fulfilled adults, members of the community rather than of an artificial sub-group linked only by the accident of handicap and partly or wholly excluded from the currents of normal living. Acceptance in the community, naturally, without embarrassment and without fuss as a person with equal rights, equal status, equal consequence is the sine qua non of full psychological health and a good self-image.

It is to be regretted that these conditions are not more often fulfilled, and, in so far as they are not, and integration is lacking, it is a symptom of undesirable attitudes among the non-handicapped. Too often, the handicapped person is treated as though he were still a child: a life-long Peter Pan deprived of adult status, of responsibility, choice, freedom of action, beholden to others and expected to obey. Parents begin the process of conditioning (not all parents, of course, but many), and it continues in a kind of tacit conspiracy by others, including very often the professional workers with whom they come in contact. It is common, too, for the physically handicapped to find themselves treated as though they were mentally handicapped also, so that, for example, a stranger will speak not to them directly but to the relative or escort with them asking about their condition or their needs. The frustrations of this type of approach (or non-approach) needs no labouring. For many people there is unquestionably a real psychological difficulty about accepting and relating to a handicapped person, particularly where the handicap is severe, involving uncontrolled movements or a speech defect. Most people get over this initial reaction fairly quickly, but there are a proportion for whom it remains a permanent barrier.

The fact that provision for the handicapped is so often in the context of charity and appeals to the public conscience is a further factor in fostering undesirable attitudes. First, it creates an image of the handicapped as a group for whom we ought to feel sorry, a group who are underprivileged and different. Attention is focused on the children, for whom it is easy to feel sympathy, even pity. Phrases like 'these unfortunate children' spring readily to the minds of those responsible for fund-raising. The feelings aroused in this way can be satisfied by giving money, and clearly no one would wish it otherwise, or object to the kindness and generosity thus shown. Nevertheless, it does create an additional psychological barrier. Giving is not relating, and it sets up a kind of non-relationship, a financial transaction of a rather impersonal nature on the basis of patron and client. Even where the benefactor gives his time as well and becomes involved personally something of the same approach will often persist, though, as I shall suggest later, real relationships can grow out of such links. Second, where less generous people are concerned, I suspect that charity appeals can cause them actively to dislike those on whose behalf the appeal is made, and to feel threatened by the multiplicity of calls on their pockets. All these attitudes militate against integration and make it more difficult for the handicapped person to find the natural, unforced acceptance as a fellow human which he has a right to expect. They are attitudes which we must do our best to minimise.

There can be no doubt that the institutional approach to providing for the handicapped has hindered, even made impossible, the development of integration. It has done this in a number of ways, but principally by the paternalistic attitudes adopted in most institutions, even the most modern and enlightened in other ways. There is an assumption, unspoken or quite explicit, that the staff and the management know best, that they have had experience of life and know the right answers, whereas the handicapped residents are inexperienced, immature, unused to the ways of the world, and incapable of sensible decisions and choices, and liable to make fools of themselves if given their head. There is a strictly communal approach to problems; the values, interests and concerns of the group are given precedence over those of the individual, and individuality becomes a liability, best suppressed, in order to preserve the peace. Signs of rebellion, even of a natural wish to assert oneself, are put down to 'being difficult', to immaturity, to a failure to fit in. We should see the failure in other terms — as a failure of the institution to recognise the person's real needs, a lack of correspondence between what he ideally wants his life to be and the reality of what society has made available for him. This is being unrealistic, of course, but in these circumstances one is tempted to say 'Long live unrealism'.

One index of the possibilities of individuality in a group is the extent to which friendships and relationships can be made outside it. Institutions are often in remote and more or less inaccessible places, far from a town — a fact which is in itself a symbol of society's caring but distant attitude to its handicapped members — and this clearly makes such contacts difficult. The communal emphasis which I have mentioned, however, is a more potent deterrent; it can be the ultimate weapon, used to discourage individual enterprise and individual links with the world outside, or indeed any individual satisfactions not shared by the group at large. 'Why should he be able to do it if the rest can't?'

Paternalism is sometimes defended, on the grounds that 'it's what they want', and perhaps the saddest aspect of these problems is that this can be true. A handicapped person of, let us say 30-35, may have had many years' experience of being treated as something less than a full adult. Vital decisions and choices have always been made for him, he has not been through the hard school of experience, he has been over-protected and cushioned from unpleasant reality, and is unaccustomed to, even in a real sense unfit for, the hazards, responsibilities and challenges of running his own life in his own way. It will be interesting to find out how far retraining and rehabilitation can be effective in preparing such a person for living in a less structured and more challenging environment.

The great danger here is apathy; the sense of purposelessness, of inability, and hence the lack of desire to shape one's life and experiences. There is the need to conform, not out of free choice as in a monastery, but because conformity is imposed from without. It is conformity, too, with a group which one may have no particular motive for identifying with other than the need for security and the continued satisfying of one's physical needs. We will all have met such people, in whom there seems to be a devaluation, a diminution of the human spirit — not, I suggest, innate and related to their handicap — but acquired as a result of their life history.

The public are in general liable to sensations of disquiet, embarrassment and even fear at the sight of handicap, particularly severe handicap. In the extreme how tempting it is to reject the whole problem and turn the other way when they are confronted by a coach-load of people in wheelchairs, with speech defects and the other manifold problems of the multiple-handicapped. Mass outings, mass events of all kinds involving the handicapped, have made the task of integration more difficult. They have their importance, of course, and have brought experiences to many that they would not otherwise have had — holidays abroad, trips to the sea, to the theatre, etc. They cannot be dismissed out of hand, but in terms of integration they are counter-productive, and not to be compared with the alternative, admittedly more difficult, of individual experience and exploration. Integration can be thought of in two phases. First, the general acceptance of the handicapped as a group (I use this phrase, I think, for the first time) entitled to a place in the community, and second, the forming of individual relationships on a person-to-person basis. The mass approach renders the first difficult, the second impossible.

In a sense, one could say that most special provision for the handicapped, in so far as it has had to deal with large numbers, has suffered from this same drawback. This is not to criticise ventures such as Het Dorp or the PHAB clubs and still less to deny their key role in providing new experiences and new opportunities, but one must draw attention to the different and special nature of them, which calls for a deliberate act of will on the part of the non-handicapped to make contact with the handicapped.

Of course, handicapped people do need special provision and special facilities, but paradoxically, their purpose should always be to enable them to approximate more closely to normality; to adapt, as it were, to their environment, so that they can live and go about their business or pleasure as far as possible unnoticed, without comment, as others do. This is the ideal for which we should strive.

If we are to achieve integration, society will have to modify many of its attitudes and traditional procedures. However, this is not to say that the handicapped person himself has no role to play in bringing it about. On the contrary, his role is a crucial one, and if I have said little about this aspect, perhaps I can emphasise it by ending with it. All that society can do is to create the conditions, the climate of opinion, the right soil, in which the flower of integration can grow. Finally, it is up to the individual to make what he can of his life, and success in integration, as in other things, depends on his own qualities and the efforts he himself is prepared to make. To be accepted, he must first accept himself as he is, realistically, and must achieve a measure of integration within himself. Upbringing and environment will both be important, since his acceptability and power to make fruitful relationships will depend on a mature, well balanced and well adjusted personality; someone who is able to ask for help and receive it with dignity, able to give as well as to receive, not too demanding of others' time and patience, not too self-centred, despite the obvious temptations of being handicapped.

Given the right soil and the right seed, as well as the right social conditions and the right outlook, the possibilities are great for creating a dignified and satisfying way of life for handicapped people who are accepted and recognised as responsible adults free from unnecessary restrictions; individuals with a sense of identity and purpose unobtrusively forming a part of the community as a whole.

21
A consumer's viewpoint

June Maelzer

I would like to start this paper with a quotation from a
gentleman who wrote to me after reading an article about me
in the *Guardian*. He is an energetic exponent of the rights of
the 'physically impaired'. He says, 'If we say that people are
human beings (a reasonable enough assumption) how can it
ever be right to exclude them from everyday life?' The
question is clearly meant to be rhetorical. This quote might,
in fact, have come from any one of a hundred or more
different minority groups — such as mental patients, the aged,
drug addicts, immigrants, and so on — all rightfully anxious
that their case for integration be recognised by the majority
at large. Indeed, in this age of mass media, facile communication — superficially at any rate — and advertising everyone
seems to be striving to reach an artificially manufactured
norm, either imposed on them by the ever more subtle
techniques of the advertising men, or a projection of their
own, often unconscious, ideals as to how society should be
properly organised. Very often their idealised and rose-
tinted picture of how the other half live bears little
resemblance to the actuality of the situation. Being aware of
the similar plights of others does not mean that one must sit
back and simply accept — on the contrary, it would be
ludicrous to starve to death in somewhere like Britain, where
food is plentiful, on account of the starving millions in the
third world. Rather strength and perseverance should be

engendered by this awareness of the similar plights of others, and a resolution should be made to better the lot of one section of the community. By this I mean that more strength and less frustration should be gained from the knowledge that there are many minority groups leading a less than ideal existence and striving to achieve better conditions and circumstances for themselves; for one group may help to facilitate the needs of society at large, rather than imagining that this single group is fighting tooth and nail for the privileges already enjoyed by the rest of society. Thus it is interesting and memorable that the Spastics Society as a corporate body — as well as individuals such as the aforementioned gentleman — should be aware of, and concerned about, the imperative need to integrate the handicapped child, and indeed the handicapped adult, into society.

Integration, for me, has two levels — namely the physical and the emotional, i.e. psychological. True integration requires the fulfilment of both of these levels. Half of the story is missed unless the latter of these requirements is recognised and attended to. I was myself very fortunate in this respect. As a child my parents were never ashamed or embarrassed about my disability. I was a child like any other child and they were, like any other mother and father, proud of me. I needed more physical help than the run of children of my age, and there was a tendency, as I grew older, to be over-protective, but my parents managed largely to resist this temptation. Nor was I 'spared the rod'. My mother's favourite phrase was 'I want her to be loved and not shunned when she grows up', and believe me I had far more thrashings than any of my friends ever did. By no means was I spoilt. It's debatable what effect it had on me, for good or ill, but I use it as an illustration of my parents' attitude towards me — I was a child like any other and had to be punished for wrong-doing as well as loved. I went to a day school for physically handicapped children, but outside school hours I was never encouraged specifically to seek the company of other handicapped

children. I played with other children in the street, who
accepted my limitations and modified games accordingly. If
there were no children around to play with I sat and read, or
did embroidery, knitting, and a hundred and one other normal
pursuits. We were a close-knit extended family, so once again
I enjoyed the company of aunts and uncles and cousins at
weekends and holidays. For me, therefore, there was never
the question of becoming integrated — I was integrated.

Ideally, of course, conferences on the integration of the
handicapped child should not arise at all; there should be no
need for them. Physical or even mental handicap should not
be looked on as abnormalities that should be isolated and
hidden away from society but merely differences that have to
be coped with in a different way, within society.

Why shouldn't handicapped children be taught with non-
handicapped children? All that is needed is a little extra
effort and positive thinking. However, the problem is not
with the handicapped or non-handicapped child, it is with the
whole educational system — too large classes, not enough
teachers, not enough specialised help or knowledge, in fact
not enough facilities. One doesn't have to be handicapped to
suffer from our system, whether educational or societal.

However, given that we are stuck with our system, at
present, small specialised groups mushroom up to help solve
specific problems. In order to offer adequate help these
problems have to be isolated and the question of integration
or re-integration arises. Just one such problem is physical
and mental disability. Today much is done to discover and
solve the needs of the handicapped who are isolated, it is
said, purely for purposes of efficiency; it is claimed, for
example, that it is easier to evaluate and implement the
needs of a hundred children in a group together than to
administer the same help to the same hundred children
dispersed amongst the population. It is difficult, in weighing
up the pros and cons of such a situation, to know whether
what is achieved in terms of help for the group is in fact

outweighed by problems of integration that are created by isolation; hence this conference.

I feel we must keep as our ultimate goal the integration of handicapped children into an ordinary school setting where adaptations are made to meet their physical needs. They can then develop and compete with non-handicapped people on an intellectual, social, emotional and psychological level. I am not suggesting it will be easy at first. Integration is interaction and interaction is a two-way process which, in turn, needs awareness. In fact, it will take a great deal of awareness on the part of the teacher, the non-handicapped child and the handicapped child. It will perhaps be easier for the children, as I believe they have a greater facility for awareness than the adult who has systematically had his awareness taken away from him and substituted by competitiveness, by the educational system and society in general, during the process of 'growing up'. It is, however, not impossible and should be constantly before us as a very real objective.

However, while this goal is being reached I feel it is imperative to cope with the present situation and to integrate the children and adults we have already isolated in our schools and homes. We must try even harder by counselling to rid parents of guilt complexes about their children's handicaps and to help them to think more positively about themselves and their children — handicapped and non-handicapped — as, I feel, integration begins in the home. A positive feeling of security and acceptance in the home goes a long way to preventing, as well as curing, emotional problems, and thus schools, whether boarding or otherwise, should have less emotional and psychological problems to cope with, theoretically. This, however, does not, in my opinion, absolve or remove all responsibility from the school and its staff. School does not simply become a learning process, in intellectual terms. In many ways it has a great deal more responsibility to the child, in its emotional, social and psychological needs than staff at an ordinary school have because of the excessive physical handling these children need. Thus the great need for security and acceptance is switched from the home to the wider social circle of school.

I feel it is imperative for 'care staff' to have specialised training in thinking of their wards as individual people with minds as well as bodies — no matter how intellectually subnormal — who have a personality, will and feelings of their own which need to be considered. All too often this is not considered — especially with adolescents and adults. This is so demoralising and tends towards depersonalisation and great problems of integration usually arising from inferiority are induced. I realise that it must sound easy for me to criticise the staff in schools and homes. However, these are not hypothetical utterances but facts. I have seen it happen time and time again to friends and acquaintances as well as little children and other people I have merely observed, besides being a victim myself although, thank God, I had achieved a firm basic security as well as an innate resilience for it not to have damaged me irreparably. I know staff are people too and cannot constantly be thinking of the child or adult, but it is important to remember that a member of staff only works a seven or eight-hour shift, whereas a child or adult has to be handled by people continuously and lasting psychological damage can be done over a period of time. By this I don't mean the handicapped child or adult must be given in to and coddled. Life is hard and they have to accept it and learn to cope with it, but a sense of reality and proportion must also be kept. Frequently, wrong areas are emphasised often for the wrong reasons. I have met many socially inadequate people working in schools and centres who desperately need to feel adequate and needed, who will constantly make comments like 'It's hard in the world you know. Nobody will help you. You'll have to manage on your own. Nobody will look after you the way I do.' This can be completely soul-destroying as well as very untrue. Of course it's not easy and one has to contemplate the possibility of being 'let down', but this just teaches one not to lean too heavily on one person and to have lots of standbys.

I strongly believe that people are basically good and, when appealed to, very accommodating. They like to be needed, and feel pleasure at being asked to help. We have not got to go far to observe this. The buildings at this conference are not purpose-built for a wheelchair! Yet I have had no difficulty at all in getting anywhere (I am not sure I can say the same for the people carrying me!) Mrs Loring told the dining room staff about me and as a result we are spoilt! Our every whim catered for — and what is more, it is obvious that they are pleased to be of help. They are being needed. I can hear you saying, 'Ah! but we are used to helping handicapped people and Mrs Loring is a representative for a conference dealing with handicapped people.' Please don't misunderstand me, I am not belittling your efforts, on the contrary I am saying that your motives are much higher. In giving one is also receiving — not that that is the reason for giving, it just happens that way, and when a handicapped person is allowed to feel a whole person, a person able to give as well as to receive, then they are well on the way to being integrated. The concept of a whole person is important for everyone to have whether handicapped or not. It is even more important to the handicapped person, because he is so dependent on other people and so vulnerable to depersonalisation and thus needs to be kept aware, at every stage of his development, that he is an individual.

It is possible, even in special schools, to arrange the curriculum to include local school children. I am sure that a good liaison with local schools is not beyond the powers of any head and his teaching staff. Integrated games time could be arranged, PE, music and movement, educational excursions to art galleries, places of historical importance, etc., and out-of-school leisure activities could be encouraged such as Guides, Scouts, Cubs, Brownies, etc. Often the school might be doing the community a service by allowing them to use school facilities which are often more abundant than in the community. In all these ways physical and emotional communication and integration could be achieved.

So often parents and adults in control are over-protective, thus harming handicapped people's ability to learn by their mistakes and stunting their development. Everyone has to learn by their mistakes, not least the handicapped. Having had experience of a tough school for the physically handicapped and a Spastics Society-run school I can say with confidence that the Society over-protect their people — not only at school but also in their homes and centres. They seem to have this precious paternalistic air which is suffocatingly damaging to personality development. It also makes it difficult to gain, and to maintain one's independence. Speaking from my own experience, which is all I can do, I am very grateful that people like Mr Doherty slip into their net, for without his quiet reassurance and belief in me as an individual, the battle to get to university would have been much harder — and believe me it was hard enough.

My university career was comparatively easy compared to my struggles to get out of the clutches of various social workers and it was only my bloody-mindedness and Mr Doherty's quiet assurance that made me achieve my goal. Now while I believe in presenting the difficulties, I also believe in positive thinking, that is to say thinking of ways of getting over these difficulties — many of which just do not exist. However, I would like to praise the Society in the monetary assistance they finally gave me and the help and assistance they are now giving me in an employment project.

I spent three very happy and socially active years at university — I'll refrain from commenting on the academic side. I had a flat and an au pair to look after me and my flat was a hub of student social life. Students came to meet and talk, to be cheered up and appreciated when they were depressed or had boyfriend or girlfriend troubles. I went to lots of parties whether in cellars or attics. I have been pushed twice on a fifty-four-mile charity walk from Lancaster to Manchester — in February! — and have been pushed half way up the Old Man of Coniston to see a waterfall. These are a few of the activities I undertook with other student friends — the people I had been told by social workers would not even have the time nor the inclination to push me to lectures. Apart from the invaluable help of all my student friends, the academic staff were wonderful. They were so accommodating and helpful throughout my three years. Ramps were built for me all over the psychology department and every effort was made to ensure that I gained the maximum benefit from the course I was pursuing.

In conclusion, two final remarks. First it is significant, and to my mind regrettable, that in a conference devoted to the integration of the handicapped individual into society so few representatives of the group of people so lengthily discussed at this conference were actually invited. Second, I would like to emphasise that my intention in this paper has been primarily a constructive, not destructive one; and my comments and criticisms have been drawn from my own personal experience, which I venture to suggest is typical of many handicapped people who have tried to break with the traditional institution and have overcome the prejudices and stereotypes of what a handicapped person must and should be like.

22
To be in society or to be beside it

Gun Andersson

Some weeks ago I had a talk with the father of a 10-year-old
boy who suffered from cerebral palsy. He was an athetoid
tetraplegic and he was attending a special class for handicapped children. I suggested that his son should try attending
an ordinary class, but the father thought that such a move
would be unnecessary as his son would never be able to hold
down a job in his own right. I thought that it was too early
to say and although I could not be certain about the boy's
future, I thought that the young boy had shown himself,
through his results at school, able to take the risk of joining
a larger group where he would certainly be more stimulated.
At this point the father asked me to list ten occupations that
would be suitable for his son. If I was able to do this, he
would be convinced of the value of moving his son to an
ordinary class. I explained that, at this stage, that was a very
difficult task.

We discussed the matter at length. The father believed that
as we progressed towards a more complex technology we
would gradually find that more and more people would be
unable to take part in the productive process. Handicapped
people would certainly fall into this category. However,
finally the father said that his son could decide for himself
whether he attended the ordinary or the special class. The
boy chose the former, but, to start with, only for a few lessons
a week. The remaining lessons he still had in the special class.

Gun Andersson

In Sweden we call this partial integration.

It is still too early to say whether this boy will be able to achieve full integration. In contrast to the father in question, other parents wonder whether the ordinary school integrates handicapped children enough. This illustrates the central issue. Should handicapped people be expected to be part of society or should they live outside the mainstream?

I am from the south of Sweden and have worked with handicapped children since 1955. In Sweden we have institutions with special classes for disabled children, most of them suffering from cerebral palsy, but we also have special classes that are integrated into ordinary schools. It is with this latter that I have worked for a long time. At present I am working as a counsellor for all special education and so do not only concentrate on the disabled.

For many years I was of the opinion, as were many other people, that the integration of the disabled child into an ordinary school was impossible. I have now changed my mind. I believe that handicapped children who have the same capacity as other children to feel, to understand, to learn and also have the same desires, wish to be with those other children in their classes and ultimately to be with them in society as a whole. They also have the right. This is what integration is about. However, I must emphasise that we should not integrate to the detriment of the handicapped person. We still need institutions and it is possible that we may never be totally without them, although we should limit the number that we build. Society has changed greatly in the last fifty years and young people who are 'different' no longer wish to be 'outside' this society.

My work as a counsellor involves three separate stages as far as the successful integration of the handicapped child is concerned:
1   Preparations.
2   Introduction.
3   Following the children once they are integrated.

The first stage has to be sub-divided into three further parts.

1a Preparations of a practical nature

I first visit the school to inspect the buildings. It would not
be very suitable if there were steps and if there are a number
of floors there must be a lift. The floors must not be too
slippery. I look at such things as the location of the toilets
and the dining-room. I may have to obtain a special desk or
chair for the classroom or even an electric typewriter. I may
have to involve myself in the choice of a suitable class and
teacher. In Sweden teachers in ordinary classes receive no
special information about handicapped children during their
training, which I think is very wrong. It should not be so, but
as a result most teachers accept handicapped children so long
as they are at arm's length. If they are placed in their own
classrooms they complain.

I also have to examine the handicapped child's transport
requirements to and from school. I may need to get a private
assistant for the child. This assistant helps the child to make
notes, to move around the school, to go to the toilet and to
help him during lunch and other breaks. It is necessary here
to expand on the private assistant's role. We need to use such
people as we also integrate severely handicapped children. We
do not believe that we should only integrate the lightly
handicapped. We have many examples of severely handicapped
children who do their work very well in an ordinary class
providing they have the help of a private assistant. The
presence of such an assistant may mean that the relationship
between the handicapped child and the ordinary children is
not all that we might desire, but the handicapped child still
wishes to be there.

1b   Information

Information should really be given to the whole society, but that is not possible at the present time. Instead I provide information to all the teachers and pupils in the schools where I propose to place a handicapped child. I also give information to the parents of the handicapped child and, above all, to the parents of the ordinary children.

I will give a few examples of what information needs to be provided and how we give it. Suppose a handicapped child is to be integrated into a first-year class. The school arranges information evenings for the parents of the beginners and I attend one of these evenings to talk about children who are different or handicapped. We then have a discussion and I emphasise that the parents have an important task in giving their children a positive outlook on their handicapped fellows. They must not keep their children away from handicapped children or they will look on handicapped people as 'curious animals'.

If the integration process is dealing with a child who has been in a special class before being transferred to an ordinary class, we usually begin with 'partial integration'; that is a few lessons a week in an ordinary class. We are able to do this as our special classes are connected to our ordinary schools. In such instances, as the initial response will not be so marked as it would be in the example above, I will visit the ordinary class and give a talk about what we mean by handicap. I may also show a short film. The children will then have the opportunity to ask questions. We finish the discussion with a visit to a special class for the cerebral palsied, where they meet a handicapped boy who uses his toes for typing. The ordinary children have never seen anything like this before and so they are quite impressed. At the same time the handicapped boy is very proud to be able to show them something that he can do but they cannot. Finally the class will meet the handicapped child who is to join their class. It is very important to ensure that this event is as simple and as natural as possible and not to make it an unusual event which would arouse curiosity.

When we are seeking full integration at the beginning of the school year, I will visit the class to tell the children about their new classmate. Parents are often present on the first day and they are, of course, welcome in the classroom. If the integration occurs in one of the higher classes, it is often useful to give the information to a wider group of pupils than just the immediate classmates.

I have to admit that we still do not provide enough information when we are integrating a child, but we have at least made a start. I also believe that it is important to provide the younger generation with information about disability. When they grow up they will be able to provide their children with the information and so the process will become continuous.

1c   The preparation for school of the handicapped child

As we have seen, there are many different types of preparation that need to be organised in order to achieve successful integration. However, we must not forget that above all we must consider the handicapped child who is being integrated. He or she is the principal person in the exercise. We must remember that he comes from a small group and that he will need a great deal of individual training, education and treatment. He must be taught about his new surroundings so that he understands the purpose of the ordinary class. He needs to be willing to make a contribution to it. We have to train him to be independent and to work at a faster rate. He will need to consider the other children and remember that the teacher has many other pupils in the class who require his attention. In short, a great deal will be demanded of the handicapped child.

The handicapped child will have to learn to fail without at

the same time giving up. He must understand that in a large
class he will certainly not be the best pupil as he might have
been in the smaller special class. He must learn that there is
something called 'competition'. If we can achieve this, or even
only part of it, we will not have forgotten the handicapped
child. He often wants to be with ordinary children; we must
teach him how to live in society and to fend for himself.

2 Introduction

The introduction can often begin with the type of information already mentioned. We can give this at the start of school-
life. Apart from this, I believe that during the introductory
period we should be in the background as much as possible.
We ought to communicate by telephone rather than in person,
although the teacher and the headmaster must know where
they can contact us, as should the parents.

It is very important that the handicapped child is allowed
to make his own entrance into his new surroundings. The
parents are often anxious that their child will not succeed,
although it is their most fervent wish — they want it as much
as their child does. The parents' anxiety can easily be transferred to the child. This is why I believe it is necessary for me
to keep in the background so that the child will not get the
feeling that when I visit the school, I do so because something
is wrong and that I am only there when help is needed. I
ought to support without being present; the child and its
parents must not be worried by the move to an ordinary
school.

It is also very important to give the teacher a helping hand.
He may need advice both of a practical and teaching nature.
He will want to know how to treat his new pupil in the best
way. The teacher must become interested and feel that he
is making a successful contribution.

3 Following the children once they are integrated

Once the initial stages of preparation and introduction are concluded we must not make the mistake of sitting back. To perform our function properly we ought to follow the handicapped child continuously, providing we have the resources. During his time at school it is important to communicate with the teacher and the school all the time. I like to participate in all the conferences at which the handicapped pupil is discussed. I then have the opportunity of gaining information about the child and also suggesting any necessary support measures. These may be on technical aspects or about communication with the various specialists concerned. I believe that the treatment team should be in the background the whole time so far as the child is concerned.

I will also have to deal with problems that arise when the pupil changes from one stadium to another, or from compulsory education to a gymnasium. I may need to recruit a private assistant and provide her with the necessary information. I may have to provide the teacher with advice or instructions when he is giving grades to his pupils.

These are the sort of areas which have to be considered when we follow the handicapped child during his school life. I should also point out here that communication with the parents is, of course, very important, as is the need to arrange for communication between school and home when problems arise.

Finally, which handicapped pupils can we integrate? I have to say that we can never generalise on this. We cannot classify handicapped children into types or degrees of handicap and then decide on that alone whether to attempt integration or not. It is often more difficult for a lightly handicapped child to manage in a large group than for a severely handicapped child. However, it is of course easier to integrate handicapped pupils with a normal intelligence than those with lower IQs. We have carried out some experiements in 'class-integration';

215

that is placing classes of mentally retarded children (not disabled) into ordinary schools, but these experiments are so recent that I cannot give any positive conclusions.

When we began to integrate cerebral palsied children, we did so in the seventh, eighth and ninth years of school. (In Sweden we have nine years of compulsory education, starting at the age of 7.) We have gradually introduced integration earlier and now we integrate cerebral palsied children direct from special nursery schools into ordinary schools. We even integrate from special nursery school to ordinary nursery school. We have found that it is an advantage to integrate some children as early as possible. We have also found that there are fewer problems in this field during the first six years at school whilst the class is kept together with only one teacher and in one classroom. The problems arise during the last three years when the system of one teacher and one class-room is abandoned. At this stage the children have to choose different courses of study in some subjects, for example, maths and English. The class then has to move to different rooms and so on. The teachers feel much more doubtful about teaching the cerebral palsied children and also giving them grades. These problems are minimised if the child has been successfully educated in the first six years.

After compulsory education ends about 85 per cent of our pupils continue their education at a gymnasium. As selection of pupils has occurred at this stage, the pupils are able to choose what they study to a large extent. Once again problems arise, but you must realise that at this stage of our development we need many more years of experience before we can make any definitive judgments.

In my part of Sweden, we have about 50 per cent of our handicapped pupils integrated into ordinary schools, but I feel that this figure is too low. During the next few years I believe that this figure will rise as we will find more pupils wanting to start in ordinary classes.

Up until a few years ago, society had no other method of

looking after and educating its handicapped children except in institutions. This almost always implied separation between parents and children and also an isolated existence. This is no longer the case. We now have greater resources and we must use them to supply alternative methods. However, it is important to remember that one method does not preclude the use of another as well. Having said that, it is possible though to decide which method we believe to be more beneficial.

It cannot be right — as I have already said — to isolate handicapped children and young people who can think, understand, feel and learn like ordinary children. Even if they know, as we do, that they cannot become fully useful members of society (that is 100 per cent productive), they still have the right to be part of society and not be to 'outside'. They want to be, and they must be, accepted as equally good fellow citizens in spite of their handicap and with their handicap. If it is necessary in such an important case to talk in money terms, this method is cheaper for society.